Signs of Intimacy

A Study in Genital Readings

by Aiden Talinggers

BALBOA.
PRESS
A DIVISION OF HAY HOUSE

Balboa Press books may be ordered through booksellers or by contacting:

Balboa Press
A Division of Hay House
1663 Liberty Drive
Bloomington, IN 47403
www.balboapress.com
1-(877) 407-4847

Because of the dynamic nature of the Internet, any web addresses or links contained in this book may have changed since publication and may no longer be valid. The views expressed in this work are solely those of the author and do not necessarily reflect the views of the publisher, and the publisher hereby disclaims any responsibility for them.

The author of this book does not dispense medical advice or prescribe the use of any technique as a form of treatment for physical, emotional, or medical problems without the advice of a physician, either directly or indirectly. The intent of the author is only to offer information of a general nature to help you in your quest for emotional and spiritual well-being. In the event you use any of the information in this book for yourself, which is your constitutional right, the author and the publisher assume no responsibility for your actions.

ISBN: 978-1-4525-7458-5 (sc)
ISBN: 978-1-4525-7456-1 (hc)
ISBN: 978-1-4525-7457-8 (e)

Library of Congress Control Number: 2013908849

Print information available on the last page.

Balboa Press rev. date: 02/09/2017

Contents

Dedication

This book is dedicated to the spirit of freedom.

May all beings be free in body, mind, and spirit.

May laughter, joy, and celebration touch your life each and every day.

Acknowledgments

I have deep appreciation for the following people, whose immense contribution made this book possible. Lani Jacobson, my sister, gave countless hours of her time helping refine the wording of the text even after it was professionally edited; she also programmed the software that allows anyone to determine their "Inner Animal Totem" and get an online reading by answering a few simple questions. Barbara McNichol, my professional editor, provided many helpful insights and solid advice. Signe Nichols, my layout editor, put everything together beautifully. Her perpetual search for excellence is largely responsible for what you see here. David Jimenez, an amazing visionary artist, brought this whole work to life with his sensitive and magical drawings. And most of all, I'm deeply grateful to you, my readers, for your courage and willingness to dive into a realm considered by many to be taboo, or just too edgy to explore with a curious mind and an open heart.

—*Aiden Talinggers*

Beginnings

A chicken and an egg lie in bed together. After a bit of time and a little rustling of feathers, the chicken turns on the light and smiles contentedly with satisfaction. Meanwhile, the egg slowly rolls out from under the covers with a disgusted look on her face and says, "I guess we finally settled that question!"

We live in amazing times. The collective wisdom of the world's unique, diverse cultures is at our fingertips via the Internet 24/7, yet the answers to these age-old questions remain elusive: "Which came first, the chicken or the egg?" Said another way, "Who am I, where do I come from, and where am I going?"

Taboos run deep in most cultures, especially around sexuality. The undercurrents of often-unacknowledged sexual dynamics become the huge-yet-invisible "elephant in the room."

But what can be more personal and central to the human existence than sexuality? Certainly, if nothing else, sexuality is essential for the continuation of personal genetics, customs, and family name.

Who Explores the Sexual Mysteries of Life?

All great civilizations have clear examples of insightful traditions that help their people make sense of their highly unpredictable world. It's striking that, with such rich and vast diversity, few of these traditions ever explore sexuality as a key to understanding the mysteries of life. They teach us to look at the stars (Astrology), our eyes (Iridology), our hands (Palmistry), bumps on our heads (Phrenology), the space around us (Auras), magical cards (Tarot decks), Yarrow sticks (the I-Ching), tea leaves, signs in nature (Omens), Ouija boards, and today's favorite, Science, to help us explain our lives—present, past, and future.

Why have almost all cultures steered away from clearly one of the most personal and sensitive reflections of our human bodies, our genitals? The questions people most commonly ask relate to love and finances. Especially when contemplating questions about love, why have we not considered exploring the most sensitive part of our body—our genitals—to gain insight into ourselves?

From science, we know that the universe appears to be dualistic; a dance between matter and energy or cause and effect. But this, in reality, is an illusion. Ever since Albert Einstein discovered $E = MC2$, we know that energy and matter only appear to be different due to their relative speeds. In fact, they are the same. What appears to be solid is made up of mostly space between the molecules; the molecules themselves have the exact same characteristics when viewed from within. Similar cascading patterns from the macrocosm to the microcosm offer a hint about the common architecture found in our universe.

Mystics have been confirming the same truth throughout the centuries—that the differences we profoundly experience are an illusion and that, in truth, we are all one. Yet here we dwell on this earth playing with language, attempting to describe things we know in our hearts are indescribable.

Life is truly a mystery, a gift to be cherished and appreciated, not a puzzle to be figured out.

The Frog's Gift of Metamorphosis

In this spirit of appreciation for the mysteries of life, *Signs of Intimacy* presents a perspective best described through a story from our frog friends. (The frog is one of the 12 Totem Animals you'll find in this book.) This story about metamorphosis (the frog's gift) refers to something that can never be fully expressed by words or captured by the inherent dualism of language. The frog's story goes like this:

At one time, the pollywogs had built a great civilization in their pond, much like humankind upon the earth today. They created wonderful places of learning, universities with brilliant teachers. Outside these institutions were a few rare beings unlike any of the student pollywogs or learned professors. Indeed, they were masters who possessed supernatural qualities and even appeared to look different from the other pollywogs. These illuminated masters would teach of a special place, another world, one they called Dry (heaven). This heaven was unlike the pollywogs' everyday world, Wet; it had air, delicious flies to eat, and many other marvelous qualities. These masters spoke of a great metamorphosis that was possible and how they too were once pollywogs.

At the same time, the leading pollywog professors of the universities in the great pond would endlessly debate with each other about the existence of such things as Dry, flies, air, and the like. You see, being pollywogs, they had no way of knowing Dry. They knew only Wet and the pond world they lived in had no word for either. As for flies, they simply did not exist. In fact, no matter how they tried to piece the words together, they could never come up with anything that resembled Dry because they were using a vocabulary derived from their known world.

4

The great professors in the universities offered seminars on this topic and wrote lengthy dissertations. However, in the end, they merely went around in circles and produced no insight at all.

The sages, on the other hand, had gone through a personal metamorphosis (awakening) and knew about Dry (heaven) from firsthand experience. Even though they could never find words in the pollywog vocabulary to describe their experience of Dry, they emanated a knowing vibration that was unmistakable. Besides, they looked different than before and had supernatural powers. They could jump huge distances that, for all practical purposes, looked exactly like flying (well, from the pollywog perspective).

The sages or ascended masters in this story teach this simple message: For transformation to occur, all that's required is faith, trust, and relaxation into one's true nature.

So as you work with the information provided here, don't get hung up on the words. They're meant to point in a direction rather than bring full understanding. Instead, experiencing the gift of life requires fully trusting in its mystery and one's inner knowing of truth.

Simply let these words wash over you and allow true mystery to arise from within.

Our World of Patterns

As cosmologists and physicists using sophisticated tools probe deeply into the physical properties of our world, well-respected philosopher-scientists have discovered that the essential nature of our universe is holographic, with its underlying design based on fractal principles. Using close observation, recurring patterns can be easily detected.

For example, on a macro level, we have the pattern of solar systems with a sun in the center and planets orbiting around it. The same pattern exists on the subatomic level with atoms comprised of a nucleus that have electrons orbiting around them. The words "as above so below" (written in the Hermetic texts found in the *Emerald Tablet*) foretold the principles of microcosm and macrocosm.

This same truth lies at the core of all divination traditions. Everything affects everything and patterns can be discerned if one studies those that emerge with enough care and insight. True art comes in knowing how to interpret these patterns as well as getting educated about the different road maps developed over the centuries.

Universally, all life is reflected within itself. To that end, patterns emerge from the initially perceived chaos. This supports the belief in a kind of higher power guiding the cosmos with an intelligence beyond our comprehension. We are not alone! Even the most brilliant scientists have come to this conclusion.

Traditional Sciences

In both India and Egypt, the science of Astrology evolved out of the fact that humans are essentially comprised of matter and water. As such, we are highly influenced by the gravitational pulls of the planets and stars. One simply has to study the changing oceanic tides to see the incredibly powerful gravitational influence of the moon. The whole ocean actually moves several feet every day.

Ancient mystics and scientists have mapped these gravitational influences. Consequently, over the centuries, complex maps have evolved showing how these influences can directly affect the lives of human beings. This, in turn, has given birth to a body of knowledge known as Astrology.

Human sexuality has always been a charged topic in most major civilizations and all too often taboo. This leaves us with few traditions to draw upon in this arena. Yes, some of the great civilizations do talk about sex and learning the art of making love, encouraging and teaching people how to become better lovers through form and discipline. For example, the Kama Sutra in the Hindu tradition is a masterpiece on learning all about the art of love. Tantra is a fantastic system for teaching the art of becoming more sensitive and less goal-oriented as a lover. In China, the Taoist sex manual *The Plain Girl's Secret Way* teaches how to conserve and gain energy in lovemaking. It focuses on the nature of yin and yang, and how these energies flow between the feminine and the masculine.

The Quodoushka teachings, derived from Native American traditions, provide a welcome exception to this masculine/feminine tradition. They've explored how the qualities of different personality types are reflected in various styles of genitalia. *Signs of Intimacy* takes this exploration into more refined definitions as well as surprising new patterns. What a fun, rich place to look for patterns—our genitals!

Signs of Intimacy shepherds a journey into "who you are" on a highly personal level. You'll be guided on a path of self-discovery, delving into your own core qualities. You'll also be invited to breathe deeply and relax into your essential nature. Not a system nor a compilation of techniques, rather, *Signs of Intimacy* is your guide to self-discovery!

Today's world seems more open and expansive than ever before. With the advent of computers and continued globalization, more knowledge can be accessed at the same time traditional taboos are relaxing, even disappearing. We're emerging from a parochial "one country—one religion—one point of view" perspective. That makes *Signs of Intimacy* extremely timely today.

My Interest in Genital Readings

During the past five years, I've become interested in this simple yet profound question: "How are the qualities that comprise our essential natures reflected in our genitals as well as in every aspect of our lives?" To investigate and gather the needed sensitive and taboo information about genitalia, I've been doing considerable "undercover research." Admittedly, much research came through on the Internet, providing access to massive amounts of information never possible until recently.

Being a student of Taoism, I took the advice of Lao Tzu and explored the "ten thousand things" of the world. This felt like a good target number to have in gathering enough raw data for my exploration. To date, I have personally viewed more than 5,000 vaginas (yonis) and 5,000 penises (linghams) to create a large enough database to facilitate the emergence of key patterns. This book documents the results of that journey.

What I love best about this book is that it has written itself. I regard it as a gift and a blessing to participate in this process, to witness life's synchronicity, and to allow nature to reveal her patterns in fun and surprising ways.

My Hope for You as You Explore This Book

Consider *Signs of Intimacy* to be only a beginning, a seed. It's my sincere desire to see this material evolve and deepen with insights and truths from many others. Over time, I'd like to see fellow explorers expand well beyond this beginning. As the great Kung Fu teacher said while pointing a finger toward the moon, "Stop looking at my finger. Look at the moon!"

Even if edgy material in this book might push a few buttons, I hope you'll always find my intentional humor within its pages as you explore what has been taboo for most of recorded time.

Although you will find many parallels to other cosmologies, you'll also find the material in *Signs of Intimacy* strikingly different. As it surprises and delights you, it gives you insight into who you are and how you can better connect with the world around you. You'll soon find yourself at the oddest moments wondering, "What kind of animal is inside this person I am talking to?" Because of *Signs of Intimacy*, you now have a fresh vocabulary to play with.

Plus you'll naturally become a better lover when you develop deeper insight into your intrinsic nature and let it empower your life. Most important, *Signs of Intimacy* promotes the art of becoming a Relaxaterian—an expert in the art of relaxing into who you are.

Rejoice in this great mystery. May your days be filled with laughter and new insights.

—*Aiden Talinggers*

Giving Genital Readings
with Skill, Humor, and Sensitivity

Three different methods are recommended for creating a genital reading. The first is the intuitive approach, the second uses the Questionnaire Form found in this book, and the third relies on physical observation. Naturally, the best genital readings employ all three methods.

To assist in your reading, have your client fill out a printed version of the Questionnaire Form. This Questionnaire Form is key to producing a quick yet high quality reading. You'll see it asks a series of questions about his or her personality qualities. Then it offers a choice of 12 drawings of different genital types, depending on the subject's gender.

The subject is prompted to circle the drawing that most resembles the physical characteristics of his or her genitals, picking second and third choices as well. For self-readings, you can find a link at the bottom of this section that has the same Questionnaire Form online. Once it's been filled out online, click on Submit, and you'll see an offer for either a Basic or an Intermediate level reading, depending on your preference.

First Method – Intuitive Reading

The Intuitive Method is accomplished by feeling the subject's animal totem essences (Primary — Inner — Further Influences) on a vibrational level. With this method, no clothing need be removed and the Questionnaire Form need not be completed. Using this method requires you to carefully observe the subject's face, body type, feet, hands, eyes, and dress. You'll also feel, on a vibrational level, what your subject's energetic signature most closely aligns with from the 12 animal totems.

Have you ever noticed people leading with one aspect of their bodies? For one person, it might be the eyes; for another, the hands; and yet another, the hair. By studying these 12 animal totem indicators described in *Signs of Intimacy*, you'll learn to intuitively pick up on which lead indicator is presenting. When you're able to perceive and note this characteristic, you'll be better able to determine which of the 12 animal totems aligns with the person's inner essence.

Using this intuitive method, there's no need to remove clothing. However, it's essential to strip your mind of extraneous thoughts. Rather than undress the person's body, undress your own mind as you follow these nine steps:

Play relaxing music (preferably with no lyrics) to cover any background noises present. Choose calming music with hints of evocative melodies and subtle instrumentation. (You can also do readings in nature if you find a comfortable place without loud noise and other distractions.)

Prepare two comfortable cushions, one for each of you to sit on, with back supports if possible. Take your places, then sit down and relax. For reference, make sure you have a copy of *Signs of Intimacy* beside you and a blank writing pad as well as a writing instrument.

Strike a brass bell or Tibetan bowl to invoke a sacred space, if you can. Invite your subject to join you in following the bell's sound with his or her attention until the sound has vanished. Strike the bell only one time. Take several deep breaths in unison while both of you clear your minds of lingering thoughts. Give yourselves time to become present with each other. Relax deeply and breathe together as one—like two seahorses perfectly synchronized in their pre-dawn dance.

After a few minutes of relaxing deeply, allow this question to arise in your whole being: "What is the Primary Animal Totem present before me in this being?" In *Signs of Intimacy*, your subject's Primary Totem is derived from the 12 different animal totems. Write down on your blank notepad the first possible animal totem that comes to you intuitively.

Close your eyes. Clear your mind with three full, deep, slow breaths and feel in your being the answer to this question: "What is the Inner Animal Totem before me in this being?" Again, write down your intuitive answer.

Close your eyes one more time and clear your mind again with three full, deep, slow breaths. Now feel in your being the answer to this question: "Are there any other animal totems partially adding their energy to either the Primary or the Inner Animal Totem present?" These are called Further Influences. Again, write down your answer(s) on your notepad. (Note: Use the convenient animal totem symbols found toward the back of this book as shorthand in notating the different animal totems present.)

Open your eyes and look into the eyes of your subject. Feel with your eyes if what you wrote still holds true. Make any changes if needed.

With your eyes still open, study your subject's body (with clothes on). Observe to the best of your ability any physical qualities that might help give further insight into the reading.

Relax and ask your subject to do something else while you compile your information to create a reading. Know that using the second and third methods will significantly add to the accuracy of your genital reading. But if you are unable to obtain either of them, then create a reading from the information you have obtained with this first method.

If you can proceed with one or both of the second and third genital reading methods, continue now. If not, skip to Organizing Your Raw Data.

Second Method – Questionnaire Form Answers and Genital Drawings Review

Have your subject fill in the Questionnaire Form and review the Genital Physical Descriptions and Drawings of the 12 different genital types for the appropriate gender. Part of the form asks the subject to pick which genital drawing and related animal totem best matches the appearance of his or her own genitals. Therefore, you'd ask your subject, "Which animal totem do you think your genitals predominantly resemble?" Also, have your subject indicate additional physical qualities that seem to be present in the Further Influences section of the form.

Third Method – Live and/or Photo Observation

Physical observation is best accomplished with photographs but can also be done live. Have your subject provide at least four "up close and personal" in-focus photos. Remember, this is supposed to be an enjoyable learning experience so make sure your subject is as comfortable as possible. Relax and have fun with the process.

For men, it's important to have photos of both an erect and a flaccid penis. It's helpful to have a number of photos taken of the erect penis looking straight on, with part of the body showing for perspective, as well as photos that show the penis flaccid. These photos will help determine the angle of the erection as well as see any tilts or curves in the penis.

For women, it's important to have photos of their labia being spread open with their fingertips as well as a number of frontal pictures with varying angles showing their labia in its natural state. It is also helpful to have a frontal picture with the subject in a standing position showing at minimum three quarters of the body. The location of the vagina in relation to the torso is often a key factor in determining the Primary Animal Totem.

When observing the genitals live, get your subject to feel as comfortable as possible. Ask if you can do anything to aid in relaxation. Sometimes offering a glass of water or a cup of tea is all that's needed.

You could shorten the time needed in the live observation by taking photos. Having photos on hand later has the additional advantage of providing a physical record for reference.

For men, as part of the reading, it's important to have an erect penis, which is probably the most sensitive issue (and tissue) that "arises." *It's strongly recommended that no touching is done unless you have two subjects who are married or in partnership.* Therefore, it falls on the male subject to handle getting an erection himself. Providing erotic photos in magazines can aid in stimulating him, but men usually know what to do.

To obtain an accurate reading, observing an erect penis provides extremely helpful data. Again, you might find taking photographs to be the easiest and best way to accomplish this. To simplify the process, you can also provide a camera so your subject can take photos privately.

Organizing Your Raw Data

If possible, combine the data from all three methods: **Intuitive, Questionnaire Form** and **Physical Observation**. However, any one or any combination will produce a satisfactory reading.

Generating an accurate genital reading requires identifying three core attributes:

Primary Animal Totem

Inner Animal Totem

Further Influences

Let's consider each of these one by one.

Determine the Primary Animal Totem from the 12 totems. Akin to the Rising Sign in Astrology, the Primary Animal Totems reflect how people present themselves in the world. After drawing on the data you've gathered through one or all three methods, choose one of the 12 animal totems that best represents your subject's genitals. Having photographs is extremely helpful in determining the subject's Primary Animal Totem. If photos or direct visual observation isn't possible, have your subject pick one of the 12 genital drawings that most resembles his or her own genitals as a second choice. If neither of these avenues is possible, rely on your intuitive feelings and the physical observations you made about your subject's clothed body. Draw together all the data available to you when selecting the Primary Animal Totem. If you have physical data from observations, photos, or your subject's selection from the 12 drawings, give these the most weight in your considerations. Your goal?

Pick the one totem that best represents your subject's Primary Animal Totem, primarily based on the appearance of your subject's genitals.

Determine the Inner Animal Totem from the 12 totems. Akin to the Sun Signs in Astrology, the Inner Animal Totems reflect the inner personality traits of your subject. Refer to your notes and review your intuitive reading. Especially note how the personality questions were answered on the Questionnaire Form. Give these answers special importance in determining the Inner Animal Totem of your subject. Each animal totem has a correlated astrological sun sign (see Animal Totems and Astrological Signs), so pay attention to his or her birth date. When determining the subject's Inner Animal Totem, follow this order of preference:

Listen to your inner guidance based on your subject's personality and indicators you have personally observed, as well as the answers on the Questionnaire Form.

Pay attention to what part of the body or being your subject leads with in the world. This can be a strong indicator of your subject's Inner Animal Totem.

If no Questionnaire Form is filled out and you do not trust your intuition, as a last resort, base the determination of your subject's Inner Animal Totem on the person's birth date and the Inner Animal correlation.

Take time to review all of your data and choose your subject's Inner Animal Totem.

Determine any Further Influences that may be present. Many genitals physically display characteristics associated with more than one animal totem. For instance, a man's penis, being large, might present predominately as an *Elephant* totem, but might have raised veins as well, suggesting *Frog* characteristics. During a woman's genital reading, you may see *Dolphin* totem mounds presenting as the predominant feature. Yet the shape of her labia may show *Snake* totem physical qualities as well. The Further Influences category allows you to weave more than one attribute into the Primary as well as the Inner Animal Totems of your genital reading, if needed. The process in determining the Inner Animal Totem Further Influences parallels the process of the Primary Animal Totem Further Influences. Carefully note if your subject is presenting any secondary personality traits and then align these qualities with the different animal totems to determine the Inner Animal Further Influences.

Be sure to include all the qualities you observe in each genital reading. Then, drawing on the available data, select the Primary Animal Totem, the Inner Animal Totem, and any Further Influences to compile a reading.

A highly accurate genital reading can be done on the computer quickly and easily. Simply go to www.SignsofIntimacy.com and fill out the Questionnaire. Click on your gender and you'll see 12 drawings of different genital types to choose from. Select the genital example that best matches you, based on your private observation. Include any Further Influences you might see present as well, and then click Submit. In seconds, you will have a complete genital reading generated by the computer.

Whether you choose to conduct your own private genital reading, rely on the computer output, or work with an experienced practitioner to receive a professional reading, you'll have an enormous amount of fun and lots of reflections to explore. Best yet, you'll have a whole new terminology that can launch you into lively conversations regarding a topic that's been taboo far too long—the proverbial elephant in the room.

Enjoy!

Animal Totems and Astrological Signs

The 12 signs in Astrology represent archetypical personality types that have been refined over the centuries. All 12 animal totems in *Signs of Intimacy* have a direct correlation to the 12 astrological signs.

By comparing your findings to Astrology, you'll discover parallels, interesting variations, and perhaps even strikingly new directions of exploration. Experienced astrologers will find themselves smiling often and saying, "I knew this was coming next!" At other times, they might say, "Now, that's really unexpected; how interesting."

Enjoy this new adventure; after all, truth is universal and the same in any language or system.

Animal Totem	Astrology Sign
Rhino	Aries (March 21-April 19)
Elephant	Taurus (April 20-May 20)
Chameleon	Gemini (May 21-June 20)
Possum	Cancer (June 21-July 22)
Tiger	Leo (July 23-August 22)
Porcupine	Virgo (August 23-September 22)
Dolphin	Libra (September 23-October 22)
Snake	Scorpio (October 23-November 21)
Frog/Toad	Sagittarius (November 22-December 21)
Turtle/Tortoise	Capricorn (December 22-January 19)
Pheasant/Peacock	Aquarius (January 20-February 18)
Seahorse	Pisces (February 19-March 20)

Three Variations of Genital Readings

In creating a genital reading and delivering it to your subject, how you convey your information is important. Consider choosing from these three styles:

1. Basic Reading

2. In-depth Reading

3. Full Professional Reading

1. Basic Reading

Read directly from your *Signs of Intimacy* book in the **Primary Animal Totems** chapter, selecting the corresponding animal totem you have chosen. First, read to your subject the description of his or her Primary Animal Totem, including both the Primary Qualities section and the In Bed section. Then read directly from the **Inner Animal Totems** chapter about the qualities of the Inner Animal Totem, your subject's **Questionnaire Form**, birth date, and/or whatever your intuition deems relevant. Add other insights that come to you and ask your subject leading questions to stimulate a dialogue. That will enrich the experience. Remember, your intention is to expand your subject's experience of him/herself and spark self-inquiry; it's *not* to categorize, define, or limit your subject's experience.

2. In-Depth Reading

Follow the instructions for the **Basic Reading** but add any **Further Influences** that contribute to your understanding. (You'll find these in the chapter on **Further Influences**.) In-depth genital readings require skill and practice. As a reader, your goal is to weave more influences and qualities into the texture of the reading, creating a deeper experience for your subject.

3. Full Professional Reading

Although similar to an **In-Depth Reading**, a **Full Professional Reading** goes a few steps further. Given in written format, it includes additional information found in the **Animal Descriptions** chapter as well as favorite Love Positions. It also pulls together a composite of these factors: **Primary Animal Totem, Inner Animal Totem,** and **Further Influences**.

The written genital reading is a personal, customized reflection of the subject. It draws on all the resources available to the professional reader, including past experiences and intuitive insights. Because the professional genital reading is highly customized, it takes time to craft it so it will reveal enriching insights. You want it to provide a pathway to deep self-inquiry and even expand consciousness by enlarging the realm of possibilities.

Remember, a genital reading is never meant to make your subject feel diminished or boxed in. Rather, it's intended to facilitate conversation about an often awkward, and sometimes taboo, area of discussion.

You'll discover that, through honest dialogue facilitated by genital readings, life can become a richer, more fulfilling experience.

Section I:

Primary

Animal Totems

Primary Animal Totems

Throughout this book, you'll see that when the personality type that refers to the totem is mentioned, the word is capitalized and in italics (e.g., *Rhino*); when the animal itself is mentioned, the word is not (e.g., rhino).

Each animal totem also has a personal reference word that can be used interchangeably with the animal totem if desired. In Astrology, someone with an Aquarius sun sign may be called an Aquarian. Similarly, in *Signs of Intimacy*, *Rhinos* can also be called Rinarians. (Author's note: These terms are made up, so you won't find them in a regular dictionary.)

This section on Primary Animal Totems can offer standalone insightful readings, but by adding the Inner Animal Totems and the Further Influences as contributing factors, a far superior genital reading will be rendered.

For your subjects to fully experience a genital reading, it's important for them to allow all the qualities within each animal totem to infuse their being. Always encourage them to allow the words in each reading to expand the vision they hold of themselves and *never* let the words diminish their sense of self in any way. Encourage your subjects to allow what feels true to grow inside of them and let the rest fade away.

Rhino (Rinarian)

Rhino: Primary Qualities

Tagline:

"Here I come, ready or not!"

Joke:

(Note: Rhinos are notorious for having poor eyesight, but they charge toward their target nevertheless!)

"Why do *Rhino* men find it difficult to make eye contact with women?"

"Breasts don't have eyes."

Rhino Genitals:

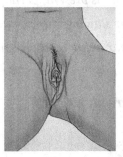 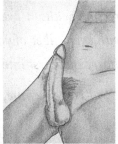

Key *Rhino* Qualities	Shadow Side
Takes initiative, Fearless	Rash, Impulsive
High self-esteem, Powerful	Pompous, Self-centered
Strong-willed, Energetic	Quick to anger, Frantic
Charges full-steam ahead, Fun	Often fails to follow through, Egotistical

Rhinos lead with their foreheads as well as their genitals!

Imagine feeling your mother's full, loving attention being focused on you as if you were the first born. Feel how all of existence is here for you, how your abundant energy arises, fueling your inspiration and life force.

Now, slowly begin to take in your surroundings. Can you feel how the desire to explore is percolating in your blood? Feel how your strong legs are moving effortlessly underneath you, almost as if they're moving on their own accord. Just for the pure exhilaration of it, you start to run as fast as you can. The increase of oxygen rushing through your nostrils inspires you, and your forward momentum allows you to run even faster. In this heightened state of physical exertion, your keen senses are hyperactive. Through your nostrils, you sense another is present; perhaps you smell your lover. Shifting direction without even slowing down, you charge toward this new energy with every fiber of your being ready to engage.

Rhinos like to charge headfirst into love.

"Here I come, ready or not!"

Rhinos tend to be adventurous, impulsive, enthusiastic, high-energy people. As lovers of freedom, they constantly explore new ideas. They often become irritated with repetition and frustrated with people they deem to be stuck in a monotonous life.

Ever enthusiastic, *Rhinos* rush into all kinds of new life experiences regarding love and business. They enjoy righting injustice. However, they often struggle with following through if they don't get quick results.

Their impatience makes it difficult for them to be consistent and hang in for the long haul. Frustrated, they can sometimes feel bogged down by the slow pace of others and the endless details of daily life.

Rhinos like to lead. They feel deeply and passionately about everything and can be effective leaders—at least, initially. Their shadow side often prevents them from capturing the hearts of their followers for sustained lengths of time.

Rhinos tend to lack sensitivity and can be unresponsive to feedback from the people they're leading; consequently, their leadership is often short-lived.

That said, *Rhinos'* ability to lead is, initially, very strong. They have the gift of feeling everything deep within their own beings and are able to transmit these feelings to others effectively. Knowing divinity from their own life's journey, they lead by example and often inspire others to find their own divine connections.

Rhinos can be strong-willed and may appear dogmatic to others because they tend to be uncompromising when it comes to their feelings.

In addition, they can be their own worst critics and spiral into depression. This usually occurs during periods of self-criticism because they don't like others to know they're thinking this way. At these times, they tend to disengage from people and demand to be left alone.

Luckily, *Rhinos* recharge quickly and seem to gather nourishment from nature as well as from physical exercise. Feeling renewed once again, the ever-energetic *Rhino* charges full-steam ahead into life's next adventure soon enough.

In Yemen, a belief prevails that the horn of the rhinoceros has magical properties and can detect poisons. It is a scientific fact that the rhino horn does react to alkalinity, and many poisons are alkaline based. When a rhino-horn dagger handle is placed into a poisoned drink, it will start to foam if an alkaline poison is present, thereby saving the intended victim's life.

Like Yemen warriors who always keep their rhino-handled daggers close at hand, *Rhinos* can discover and eliminate their own toxic ways of thinking with their intrinsic rhino-horn qualities. *Rhinos* have a keen ability to detect lies when communicating with others. By using this same truth detector for self-reflection, their own innate honesty can act as a rhino-horn litmus test and pull them out of toxic thinking patterns into a more positive perspective. It's important for *Rhinos* to remember that their toxic thinking detector is always available, even in their darkest hour.

Highly protective of their children, often *Rhinos* would rather die themselves than see harm come to their children. They may go to extreme lengths to support them, and they'll usually choose their children over any other relationship.

Extremely physical, *Rhinos* enjoy making love, dancing, sports, yoga, performance, and doing physical work. Because they like to stay in shape and exercise frequently, they tend to be good athletes.

Although *Rhinos* don't always see clearly, like their animal totem, the rhino, they have keen senses of smell and hearing. If people talk about them quietly under their breath, *Rhinos* always hear it—and can become rather reactive if they don't like what they hear.

Rhinos tend to have strong impulses to act quickly and are also drawn to fire. The Malaysians have a wonderful legend about how the rhino will suddenly rush in to stamp out a kindling forest fire (as seen in the movie *The Gods Must Be Crazy*). Sometimes, *Rhinos* will stamp out their own fire by acting too impulsively in their constant search for novelty and adventure.

Rhinos in Bed

Rhinos love to jump right in, charging head first into love. They abound with energy, are often the life of the party, and love to be physical. Like the rhinoceros, *Rhinos* usually have poor eyesight. They tend to be impulse driven and easily get drawn into fantasies. They don't like being called on their "stuff" and often move on, rather than work on their "issues."

Sexually, *Rhinos* often rush into relationships and tend to be impulsive, which can lead to quick decisions such as getting married after knowing someone for only a few days or weeks. This same impulsive quality can also lead to having affairs and going through phases of promiscuity.

Rhinos like to make sounds when having sex and are very expressive. Grunts, loud breathing, and occasional shouts are common. With their playful, creative nature, they tend to be attentive, sensitive lovers. Direct about their intentions, they often prefer oral sex and are skillful with their hands, although they love getting physical in any configuration. They're among the most fun-loving sex partners of all the totems.

Rhinos enjoy leading the way and can bring deep feeling and passion into their sharing. Their lovers tend to be swept into the excitement and carried along in it, getting them in touch with their own passions along the way.

In addition, *Rhinos* are usually quite attractive, many enjoying thick, lustrous hair. Having both good appearance and a high level of fitness is important to *Rhinos*, and they usually want their partners to be in good shape as well. Great kissers, they love being direct and personal, face to face. They often have a powerful impact on their lovers.

At the same time, *Rhinos* can be quite changeable. They tend to charge into whatever passion they're feeling in the moment and can easily change direction—just as a charging rhino can turn on a dime and forge ahead in a new direction. This can be painful for their lovers who usually don't see it coming. They can't understand how their *Rhino* lover who felt so passionate about them only a few days ago may already be out exploring with someone else. At these times, *Rhinos*—whose basic nature is to tell the truth—may be too embarrassed by their own actions to immediately come clean about what's going on. Eventually, though, they tell the truth because being straightforward is their true nature. *Rhinos* can sometimes forget to practice safe sex when moving too fast, so asking the question is always important.

Rhinos often find it difficult to stay in a relationship for the long haul. They tend to lose interest and become disappointed when they feel that their lover is stuck in one particular way of thinking. Charging on ahead, the *Rhino* persona continually looks for new experiences, always asking the question, "What else is possible?"

Rhino's Higher Octave

The basic nature of a *Rhino* is impulsive and changeable. At core, they are full of life and passionate about everything. The invitation for the evolving *Rhino* is to use their own life experiences as learning opportunities, and to slow down and remember to breathe. Finding rhythm in their lives and placing their awareness on their breath can be powerful tools to help *Rhinos* evolve to a higher octave. *Rhinos* are born with an abundance of energy and passion. Perhaps it's by allowing their charge-head-first energy to express itself fully, while at the same time becoming more aware of how they affect others, that the *Rhino* truly transforms. The evolved *Rhino* places his gaze on a wider field of vision, allowing more to become possible. In this way they discover… through eyes wide open, they truly see!

Elephant (Elephantarian)

Elephant: Primary Qualities

Tagline:

"You're never going to forget me!"

Joke:

"What did the elephant say to the naked man?"
"How do you breathe through that small thing?"

Elephant Genitals:

 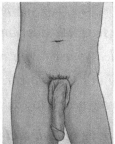

Key *Elephant* Qualities	Shadow Side
Big, Strong	Slow, Docile
Patient, Determined	Petty, Controlling
Relaxed, Confident	Rigid, Angry
Warmhearted, Caring	Possessive, Resentful
Intelligent, Has a Good Memory	Jealous, Self-absorbed

Elephants lead with their ears (hearing)!

Imagine feeling totally comfortable inside your own skin and the world at large. Can you sense how you are special, how you are bigger, energetically, than most other people?

Notice where you're holding tension in your body. Can you let go, relax a little deeper? Take a deep breath and exhale slowly. Scan your body with your awareness again. Are there any changes taking place? Somewhere inside, you sense that the more you can relax, the more you will be given. Can you sense how genuinely comfortable you are in being just who you are? Elephants are true Relaxaterians.

You've surrounded yourself with beauty; your home is full of treasures. Love comes to you of its own accord; you needn't pursue it. Can you feel your beloved drawing nearer to you now? You are irresistible.

"Here I am. I am beautiful, and you're never going to forget me!"

The sheer size of elephants—whether physical or energetic—can be impressive. Often bigger than life, their hugeness can be about their heart or around their loyalty to friendship, even after many other friends have disappeared. Elephants tend to have a grace and ease about them that can be surprising given their large (physical or energetic) size.

When the *Elephant* appears in a reading, it often indicates the qualities of grandness, patience, slow deliberate intelligence, and comfort in one's own skin.

Elephants exude an easy-going feeling and tend to be far less judgmental, fearful, or agitated than many other animal totems. This is often due to their larger-than-life presence, both physically and emotionally. They tend to grow up feeling secure and unthreatened, which creates a kind of psychic spaciousness during their developmental years. This feeling fosters confidence and a genuinely friendly, relaxed attitude, especially with people of their own social strata—their tribe (herd). Because they prefer to mingle with others they perceive as being part of their social crowd, at times, people who aren't part of their circle may experience them as snobbish or cliquish.

Elephants are practical, steady, reliable, and usually self-contained. They have incredibly thick skins (one inch thick on a real elephant, to be exact) and don't get caught up in the small details of life. But if pushed too far, their anger can be horrifying.

They're not generally known for being adventurous, but in spite of their often big size, they're incredibly sensitive, which may show up in the form of artwork. Artwork? Yes. Even real elephants can be artistic. Perhaps the most famous elephant artist in history was Ruby, an Asian elephant who lived at the Phoenix Zoo in Arizona (from 1973 to November 6, 1998). She became a worldwide sensation by creating incredibly sensitive and delicate artwork that rivaled some of the best modern art. Ruby's paintings fetched as much as $25,000 dollars for a single painting, and she often produced more than a $100,000 in artwork each year. When Ruby died in 1998, more than 48,000 people came to commemorate her life.

Ruby is not alone in the art world; today many elephants paint. Their paintings have been shown in museums and galleries around the world, and some elephant paintings are even sold at famous auction houses such as Christie's.

Like Ruby, *Elephants* love beauty. They're attracted to beautiful people and beautiful things. They also love pleasure but have a tendency to overindulge, which makes them susceptible to the overuse of drugs, alcohol, and food. They can overindulge in sex and sexuality as well; at times, they can even show hedonistic characteristics.

Sometimes, though, *Elephants* take the opposite tack, diving deeply into their spirituality; renouncing drugs, sex, and materialism all together with the same zealous spirit.

Elephants like things orderly, but they're not hung up on cleanliness. In fact, they like getting dirty. For them, dirt is synonymous with the earth—and they're all about their connection to the earth. The earth is an *Elephant's* (as well as elephant's) greatest ally. Fortunately, the earth is usually accessible, and a deep connection with it always brings *Elephants* back into balance. Feeling connected to the earth as well as to their tribe (herd) provides immense healing and centering for them.

Real elephants also have a strong connection to the earth. Often observed in the wild with their trunks pressed to the ground, elephants are listening for their companions far away. Through their trunks, they can literally feel/hear the low vibrations of their herd's footsteps through the ground up to five miles away. This illustrates how significant an elephant's connection is to both the earth and its family members.

Elephants make relaxed, faithful lovers and partners because they're slow to anger and aren't easily disturbed. They rarely entertain thoughts of doubt and will give the benefit of any doubt to their friends and partners.

However, if a betrayal becomes inevitable, watch out! All hell can break loose. Anger, jealousy, and resentment can rear their ugly heads. Then the normally phlegmatic *Elephant* suddenly becomes a raging bull *Elephant*. (Elephants can't see clearly, and when they're enraged, steer clear of them because just about everything in their pathway will be leveled.) Fortunately, it takes a lot to provoke *Elephants* enough to reach their boiling point!

Although generally relaxed, in relationships, *Elephants* can become controlling; they like being king or queen of their domain. With their tendency to be possessive, they all too often want to orchestrate the lives of their partners and children.

Elephants prefer their mates and family members to align with their own concepts of religion, ideology, and politics. When nonalignment arises, problems can develop because of this sensitivity. They clearly want the people close to them to be in alignment with their views and that of their tribe (herd).

Almost universally, elephants have been associated with good luck and fortune. Popular in India, Ganesha (the Hindu elephant god) has a human body and an elephant's head. Representing wisdom, Ganesha is believed to shatter all obstacles to the flow of financial abundance and good fortune.

Elephants possess a range of qualities that are more diverse and clearly defined than those of many other animal totem personas. Humans are always far more than the sum of our individual parts. Remember the famous Indian fable about the four blind men describing an elephant? Each was able to perceive only one aspect of this huge animal when touching him. For the blind man touching the elephant's side, the elephant was a wall. For the second blind man feeling its trunk, the elephant was a rope; for the third blind man touching the elephant's leg, it was a tree trunk; and for the fourth blind man touching its ear, the elephant was a fan. This fable teaches that our perceived reality makes up only a small part of the true picture, certainly not the whole.

From our elephant friends, we know that we're much more than the sum of our parts. Let's celebrate this quality as a gift and allow these words to expand our understanding of ourselves. Life is so much bigger than we're ever able to imagine.

Elephants in Bed

When in bed, Elephants are relaxed and comfortable in their own skins. Sexually, they tend to be steady and long lasting, allowing the sexual energy to build up slowly. As confident and patient lovers, they like to take their time. They tend to be quiet by nature, but when stimulated, they may "trumpet" their excitement with enthusiasm and considerable loudness.

Because of their poor eyesight, *Elephants* tend not to get hung up on how their lover looks; they're much more concerned with how they feel and smell.

Highly loyal, *Elephants* aren't drawn to being promiscuous. Being quite steady, they shy away from changeable people and circumstances, finding deep pleasure and peace in consistency. Simple in their hearts, *Elephants* aren't interested in intrigue and certainly don't want any complexities arising from love.

Elephants have amazing memories. With their ability to remember everything, *Elephants* can hold all the love they've ever experienced in their hearts. Because of that, the present moment is connected to all of eternity. Within the *Elephant's* heart, time and space collapse, becoming one with all of existence.

Elephant's Higher Octave

It's basic nature for *Elephants* to be steady and easy going. At core, they are comfortable with themselves and with living simple lives. The invitation for evolving *Elephants* is to learn through their own life experience and to branch out and take more risks. Experiment, change things up a bit and see where it takes you. You may be pleasantly surprised with the results. Letting go of strong beliefs and ingrained concepts can initiate powerful explorations which help *Elephants* evolve to a higher octave. *Elephants* are born with steady, reliable natures. It's by allowing their consistent personality to express itself fully, while at the same time taking new risks and exploring new possibilities, that *Elephants* can truly evolve. By placing their gaze in new directions such as experimenting and breaking out of social molds, so much more becomes possible. Flexible minds rarely break—and besides, the unknown is quite often exhilarating!

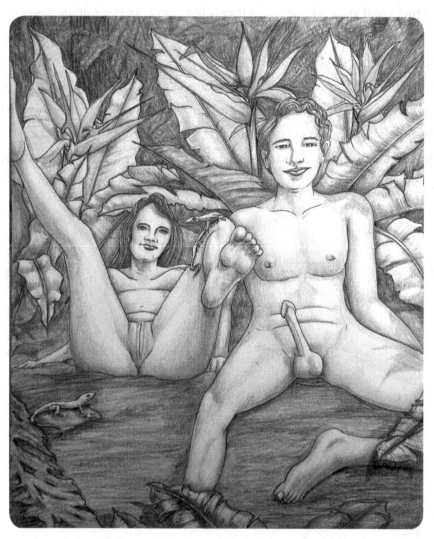

Chameleon (Chamelaterian)

Chameleon: Primary Qualities

Tagline:

"Catch me if you can."

Jokes:

"What does the Zen master say to the *Chameleon* hot dog vendor?"
"Make me one with everything."

The Zen master has only a 20-dollar bill so he asks the *Chameleon*
vendor, "Can you make me change?"
The *Chameleon* immediately pockets the 20 and answers, "Change
yourself; change comes from within."

Chameleon **Genitals:**

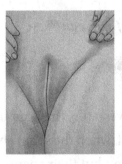

Key *Chameleon* Qualities	Shadow Side
Camouflage ability, Versatility	Nervous, Distracted
Inquisitive, Curious	Mental, Self-absorbed
Multi-tasking, Talkative	Inconsistent, Shallow
Good Communicator	Changeable, Hidden
Youthful, Energetic	Tense, Sleepy

Chameleons **lead with their minds!**

Feel the quicksilver electric energy vibrating in your body. Imagine mercury with its silver brilliance, its liquid nature that can so easily slip through your fingers. Notice how sensitively it reacts, like a thermometer, sensing the slightest increase in temperature, expanding and rising—just like warm blood flowing into your secret places.

Can you feel how your loins tingle with this life-giving, electrifying energy?

Just as quickly as you respond to the heightened energy surrounding and filling you, you can feel yourself cooling down again with the ever-changing moment-to-moment movement of life. Your eyes scan the horizon now, eager to experience life's next wild adventure.

"Catch me if you can!"

Because *Chameleons* are extremely versatile, they can blend with many diverse situations. Like a smart lizard, when the sun is shining, they soak up its warmth and abound with energy, but their energy wanes when the source is gone.

Chameleon personas tend to draw sustenance from each new person they come in contact with, blending again and again with what is new. It's not in their nature to be the center, the source; rather, they prefer to reflect another's energy. Like their chameleon animal totem that has skin that reflects light and changes color to merge with its environment, *Chameleons* use a similar reflective quality to blend in as well.

This changeability can cause a lot of trouble in the emotional world. *Chameleons* often appear to be flighty and can be hurtful when in relationship with animal totem types who desire constancy and dependability. To some, *Chameleons* might seem cold hearted or even cold blooded in their shifting allegiances. From their own perspective, though, *Chameleons* are merely adjusting to their environment to survive. They often don't understand the pain their loved ones feel when affected by their changeability and instinctual need to be in the presence of continually new sources of energy.

Like their chameleon totems, *Chameleons* are often dazzlingly attractive, wearing vibrant colors and beautiful clothes, giving them great appeal in others' eyes. *Chameleons* are often the objects of desire.

Intelligent, they can become strongly stimulated in the presence of other intelligent beings. They love to reflect that energy by engaging in lively conversation. Their active minds often lead them into verbal sparring, which can quickly become a mental ping pong game. They love quick exchanges and have incredibly fast and agile minds as well as tongues.

When a real chameleon is hunting, its tongue can strike out faster than the human eye can see—at about a 30 thousandths of a second. How's that for fast talking?

For all their intelligence, *Chameleons* often appear to lack depth because of their changeable nature. Their intellect is keenly analytical, which gives them the ability to see both sides of any argument, thus making it hard for them to stay with one perspective and be decisive.

Chameleons are enthusiastic and love to get involved. Yet because they have trouble sticking with things, making lasting decisions can be particularly hard for them. They tend to charm others and, at their best, rely on their attractive looks, quick wittedness, authenticity, and straightforwardness. At their worst, they can slip into sulking, complaining, being evasive, and blaming others.

Real chameleons have the ability to rotate their eyes 360 degrees. When their eyes are spun halfway around, the lizards appear to be looking back into themselves, almost as if they're meditating. Having observed this trait, Native Americans created many stories about chameleons having one part of their essence living in the dream world.

Just like their animal totem, *Chameleons* often have one eye looking toward this world and one eye perceiving the dream world. It's essential to understand his dual nature if you want to grow close to a *Chameleon.*

Interestingly, chameleons appear to be unreliable in mythology as well. The Bantu people of South Africa tell this story about the chameleon: Being the dreamer that the chameleon is, he became a messenger for God (Unkulunkulu) and was sent to carry an important message for mankind between the worlds. The message that the chameleon was supposed to give to the people was "Man shall not die." Well, being who he was—self-centered—the chameleon dawdled. He took so much time eating food and resting along the way that God's message didn't reach the people in a timely fashion. Knowing that, God sent a second messenger with a different message that said, "Man shall die!" The second messenger didn't dawdle at all, traveling fast and arriving first. When the chameleon finally arrived and delivered his message, it was too late. Fear had already taken hold. The people believed the first message they received, so today people die and don't live for eternity. It was the chameleon's self-centeredness and habit of distraction that caused this tragedy.

Like the chameleon in this story, *Chameleons* are rarely punctual because they're easily distracted.

Chameleons in Bed

Chameleons love to share intimately and are usually highly energetic lovers. Curious about new ideas, they're often open to experimenting and discovering new ways to make love. They're drawn to high-energy lovers and gather a lot of their excitement from their partner's electricity. Often, *Chameleons* simply respond to another's attraction and energy by reflecting it back in all its splendor and intensity. Rarely do *Chameleons* initiate.

Chameleons love the chase, but they're hard to catch and, like most lizards, sometimes sacrifice their "tails" to eventually get away. Beware. Just because a *Chameleon* makes love with you doesn't mean you've captured his or her heart forever. *Chameleons* often just give a little "tail" so they can make a clean getaway a while later. Don't be surprised if you wake up in the morning with a pleasant note on your pillow rather than the beautiful head that rested there the night before! Welcome to the ever-changing world of the *Chameleon*.

Chameleons respond best to a catch-and-release strategy—the kind that fishermen employ when fly fishing. Hold on too tight and they'll run away; give them lots of room and they tend to circle back for more. *Chameleons* can't resist the energy of unconditional love. Just as the sun rises every day and warms the earth, they'll return to gather the new energy you have to give. Then they'll reflect it back to you in all their splendor and brilliance.

Chameleons can appear fickle, but often their unpredictability has more to do with having one foot in the dream world as well as one foot in this world. Seeing *Chameleons* in this light will enhance one's ability to understand them and grow closer. *Chameleons* can be viewed as passing between this world and the dream world in their ability to change color and melt into the background—their ability to disappear. Those who see and value this quality will be amply rewarded for their expansive vision and ability to be open minded.

Chameleon's Higher Octave

Chameleons tend to be fickle and changeable. At core, they are comfortable with an ever changing environment and intense dynamics with others— especially intimates. The invitation for the evolving *Chameleon* is to learn through their own life experiences; to slow down little by little and deepen their connection to their own inner dream world. By placing their gaze on their own rich interior world, they can begin to find an internal source of light and a direct connection to God.

You may be pleasantly surprised by what you find. Shifting to a more balanced life, as an evolved *Chameleon*, you can retain your ability to reflect another's brilliance, but at the same time stay in touch with your own divinity and emanation of light. Perhaps in this way you can begin to experience the next octave. It's by allowing your own natural flexible personality to express itself fully, while at the same time remaining centered in your own being, that new possibilities can truly emerge.

The movement of a spinning record best illustrates this evolution. The outer edge of the record spins fast, while the center remains almost still. Yet it is the same record. Where we place our attention determines how we experience life. The evolved *Chameleon* moves his gaze continually towards the center of his life. Soon, what was once perceived as moving so fast, slows down as the center is approached and eventually reached... *arriving at the center, the still point ... a place of peace and equanimity.*

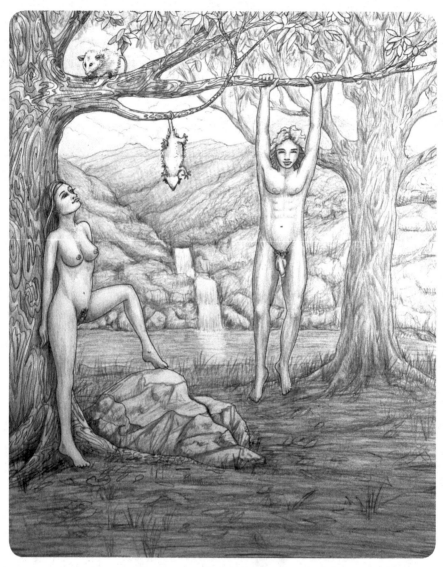

Possum (Possairian)

Possum: Primary Qualities

Tagline:

"Where is my Prince Charming? I will love only the perfect one!"

Joke:

"What's better than roses on your piano?" "Tulips on your organ!"

Possum Genitals:

 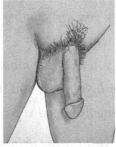

Key *Possum* Qualities	Shadow Side
Loving, Intuitive	Fearful, Clingy
Emotional, Deep-feeling	Moody, Touchy
Protective, Careful	Defensive, Attached
Shrewd, Intelligent	Changeable, Self-destructive
Youthful, Energetic	Tense, Sleepy

Possums lead with their hands!

Imagine the moon is shining through your window right now. Can you feel her fullness, her roundness, spilling into your very being? A kind of lunar madness arises within you, stirring your juices, filling the air with laughter and light.

Then the moon shifts. Only a crescent fingernail-sliver of light passes through your window now. It's a time of hiding, of fading into the silvery twilight found between dimensions.

Can you feel how you are slipping even deeper into total darkness with the coming of the new moon?

Look closer and you'll see the moon hanging in the night sky. No longer illuminated by the light of the sun, the moon has become a phantom, a silhouette, appearing like a faded pastel, but still present.

"Ever patient, I wait for my princess (prince) before emerging from the shadows yet again.

Just like the moon . . ."

Possums are ruled by the phases of the moon and embody all these qualities. At times, they may appear asleep, dead to the outer world. But inside, they are fully present, waiting, watching—just as the new moon seems to wait and watch. It's interesting to notice that what changes is the light of the sun and how it strikes the moon's surface, not the moon itself. Welcome to the ever-shifting atmosphere surrounding the inner world of *Possums*. They can be quite moody, and their mood shifts are clearly expressed on their faces, reflecting exactly how they feel.

Possums tend to be shy and withdrawn, but at times, they can be brilliant, even captivating. They are often lovers of coffee or tea because caffeine tends to amp up their energy a notch.

Possums rarely seek the limelight. Rather, they love their home life. While they're good organizers and housekeepers when engaged in big projects, *Possums* tend to be messy on a day-to-day basis.

Energetically, they love things that are old and often surround themselves with objects they strongly associate with significant memories. Due to their uncanny memories, *Possums* remember everything that has ever happened to them—down to the smallest detail.

Possums tend to view the world from an uncommon perspective. At their worst, they're too eager to point out the injustices of the world. But at their best, they're brilliant and truly see many things that others don't. It's almost as if they have the ability to hang upside down by their prehensile tails like their possum totem to gain unique insights from this radicalized, inverted vantage point. This aspect of the *Possum* echoes an archetype found in the Native American tradition of the Heyoka (the Trickster). He offered insightful, unique perspectives about important matters of life—often from a highly unconventional vantage point.

Sexually, *Possums* tend to have a reduced sex drive—or a drive that ends at a much earlier age than for most people. *Possum* females may simply lose interest in sex for no apparent reason, possibly reaching menopause (men–o–pause) at a younger age than women of other animal totems.

Possum men may have difficulty achieving erections during lovemaking sessions. They also may seem to have a lower sex drive or lack interest compared with other men. It's striking how much earlier *Possums* lose interest in sexuality than do other animal totem personas. In part, this may reflect their inherent desire to focus their vital energy on spiritual pursuits.

Science teaches that energy can never be destroyed, only transformed, just like a light bulb's light energy transforms itself into heat. The same is true with the *Possum's* sexual energy, which naturally shifts into spiritual pursuits. *Possum* personas prefer to build a strong spiritual connection as a foundation before entering into sexual relationships.

Animal possums possess a characteristic rarely found in other segments of the animal kingdom called senescence or rapid biological aging. The word *senescence* is derived from the Latin *senex* meaning "old man" or "advanced in age."

Possums seem to be old souls with a similar characteristic manifesting in their sexual drive. *Possums* sometimes allow their fears to take over. They too easily identify with old, deeply entrenched fears, which may play a part in their desire to hide and not be sexually available.

Possums in Bed

In love, *Possums* have learned to phase like the moon, reflecting the light they sense is emanating toward them. Shy creatures, they prefer to make love at night when the lines between shadow and reality blend and everything is shrouded in veils of darkness. Because they often prefer to hide, they like the cover of darkness.

Possums tend to be fearful. They often feel vulnerable and can present an outer persona of low self-esteem. Inside, though, they have a strong sense of themselves and an internal compass that guides them with true conviction.

Possums can feel threatened when pursued romantically because they often have deep-seated wounds from the past that affect how they feel consciously—as well as subconsciously—about themselves. *Possums* might appear to play dead at these times. *Possum* women might find it difficult to orgasm, or they could completely lose interest in sex all together. *Possum* men might have difficulty achieving erections, tending to lose their desire before things heat up, or they may ejaculate too soon. Their genitals may appear to be dead at these times, but they're just playing possum!

It's essential for *Possums* to learn to be more open about what goes on for them emotionally and share their true feelings. In learning how to be more honest, everything can begin to change for the *Possum* and so much more becomes possible. For example, there are many more exciting and different ways to make love than the standard missionary position. When a *Possum* totem starts thinking outside the box, watch out. Things can get more exciting than your wildest fantasy.

Possums often have deep spiritual natures and need to feel connected in this realm before they can open up physically.

Archetypically, *Possum* personas can be seen in the stories of Snow White and Sleeping Beauty, both of whom were awakened by their princes after being asleep for a long time. Snow White falls into a deathlike (possum) sleep after eating a poisoned apple given her by the disguised evil queen, only to be later awakened by the kiss of her true prince. This classic fairytale presents an interesting paradox with respect to the *Possum* archetype. Much emphasis is placed on Snow White appearing dead while awaiting the kiss of her prince. Yet, what about all the time before Snow White eats the poison apple? By far the biggest part of the story depicts Snow White bubbling with life, singing, laughing, and enjoying her friendships with the Seven Dwarves.

What does this teaching tell our present-day *Possums*? Even though *Possums* are perpetually awaiting their princes and princesses, they can (and often do) have happy lives filled with diverse friends (dwarves).

These friendships can be quite satisfying, and the true value of friendship appears to be far underrated. For *Possums*, rethinking their own archetype can prove to be self-empowering.

It takes tremendous sensitivity and perseverance to break through a *Possum's* challenging defenses, but once they're pierced, excitement follows. Loving by nature, *Possums* enjoy expressing themselves sexually, especially when they feel safe.

With their 50 teeth, real possums show their affection with love bites, just as *Possums* enjoy expressing their love with endless passionate kisses. Like their animal totem with prehensile tails, *Possums* love to explore creative new positions in lovemaking. You might find them hanging off the chandeliers or certainly the bedposts. They tend especially to love receiving and giving oral sex.

Once Prince Charming or Princess Perfect gets past this archetype's formidable defenses, *Possums* make loyal, dedicated partners. Committed parents, they fiercely protect their young. *Possums* enjoy nurturing their families and have a deep need for a sense of home. Like their animal namesake that carries its young in a pouch, "home" is always present at the center of their existence.

Possum's Higher Octave

Possums tend to be fearful and cautious by nature. At core, they like to hide and remain in the shadows, often finding that they are left with aloneness and separation. The invitation for the evolving *Possum* is to learn through their own life experience to trust more often and to spend less time hiding.

By simply revealing who you are, you will find that possibilities begin to emerge. You may be pleasantly surprised by what the universe begins to offer you. Letting go of your strong beliefs and ingrained concepts can initiate a powerful exploration that helps you evolve to a higher octave. *Possums* are born with fearful natures. It's by allowing your natural skepticism to express itself fully, while at the same time beginning to take new risks and exposing your true feelings, that you will truly evolve. Perhaps by placing your gaze on what feels good, rather than on what might go wrong, new and different outcomes may become possible. In the presence of love and light, an expanded truth will inevitably be revealed.

Tiger (Tigarian)
and *Other Big Cats*

Tiger: Primary Qualities

Tagline:

"I am adorable. Love me!"

Joke:

"How do *Tigers* describe themselves?" "Purr-fect!"

Tiger Genitals:

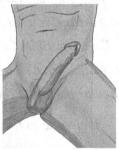

Key *Tiger* Qualities	Shadow Side
Heart-full, Loving	Dogmatic, Controlling
Patient, Persevering	Pompous, Egotistical
Show leadership, Confident	Moody, Cunning
Broad-minded, Caring	Possessive, Resentful
Creative, Enthusiastic	Jealous, Self-absorbed

Tigers **lead with their hearts!**

Can you hear that soft, melodious purring sound penetrating the forest night? Tiger is on the move again, coming closer, eyes ablaze. Can you feel how your attraction grows like a wave of hot animal magnetism in your bones? Your skin tingles with a warm fuzzy feeling that, inch by inch, moves down into your loins, stirring a wild electricity you can barely contain.

Imagine you are in the jungle now—lush, wet, hot, teeming with rich smells, colors, and wild sounds. Can you feel how your whole body has caught fire? As if in a dream, you hear Tiger's voice softly yet forcefully echo inside your head. "I'm irresistible. Come love me!"

Before you even realize what's happening, from under the leafy green canopy a sleek muscular body flies through the air toward you.

Welcome to this Tiger's world!

Tigers are romantic and passionate about many things, especially love.

Exploring the qualities of tigers touches on the whole family of Big Cats, including lions, cheetahs, cougars, jaguars, and panthers. The core Big Cat—the tiger—exhibits qualities common to all, and hence is the primary subject here. Each subspecies has essential variations to consider, which are also described. If you think one of these other cats provides a more accurate description, be sure to incorporate these qualities into your reading as well.

Tigers love to be the center of attention. Attuned to the sun, they reflect its central position in our solar system. Commonly, they make good leaders and are usually well loved. Their universal magnetism fosters loyalty and admiration from many. *Tigers* have the innate ability to be chivalrous; their natural enthusiasm inspires others.

However, when *Tigers* slip into their shadow side, they can become pompous, self-aggrandizing, sexually out of control, autocratic, and loud—often resorting to yelling. Fortunately, *Tigers* rarely behave this way because they have an acute need to be loved and adored. They also have an active self-witness that helps keep them thinking positively.

Tigers can be goal oriented and are often driven. Sometimes, they become fixated on a project. When this happens, people close to them (especially loved ones) can feel disconnected if they're not directly involved in the project.

Quite simple by nature, *Tigers* respond favorably when they're gently reminded to stop being fixated on work and pay better attention to their loved ones. This helps them refocus on their heart connections. They like being encouraged to share in love; they experience a feeling of being wanted and a sense of coming home.

Tigers tend to be open and transparent. They dislike secrets and anything that's not forthright. For this reason, they make bad confidants. They also have poor memories, so simply telling the truth is best when communicating with *Tigers*. The *Tiger's* strong preference for honesty and directness generally stems from a desire to make life simpler rather than addressing a moral issue.

Tigers tend to like themselves and have a natural desire to be seen; they're not wired to live in a world of secrets and intrigue. Indeed, their innate raw animal power affords them the dignity to stand up and be seen for who they are.

In the Aesop fable "The Lion and the Mouse," the lion represents his Big Cat brothers and sisters. Early one morning, a sleeping lion was awakened by a small mouse crawling up over his body. The lion immediately grabbed the small mouse, held him up by his tail, and exclaimed, "I am going to eat you!"

The frightened mouse said, "Please don't eat me! You never know—I may be able to save your life someday."

The lion laughed heartily at such a preposterous idea and replied, "Now you've made me laugh so hard, I can't eat you, so I will have to let you go."

Only a few hours later, the great lion was caught by hunters and tied up. The small mouse chewed the lion's restraining ropes until he cut through, setting the surprised and thankful lion free.

Moral? One never knows what can happen so it's important to be kind—always. And for all their intensity, *Lions* as well as *Tigers* are, more than anything else, kind-hearted.

Tigers in Bed

Tigers love to be naked—to stretch out in the sun and soak in life. They tend to sleep peacefully and enjoy awakening in the early morning, reveling in the sound of whispering leaves and singing birds. They feel most at home in nature but can adapt well to cities, too.

As lovers, *Tigers* are full of energy and passion. They can become quite preoccupied when sexually enamored. Acting like their Big Cat friends, they tend to pounce on their objects of affection with total abandon, drawing their lovers into their own level of passion. On their shadow side, *Tigers* can become imbalanced quite easily and spend inordinate amounts of time and energy playing in this sexual arena. You might hear a *Tiger's* lover say, "Okay, it's time to get out of bed already!" But just as often, the *Tiger's* lover makes no protest, having already been happily drawn into the sexual play.

All about love and living in their hearts, *Tigers* can't resist their attractions. They show keen interest and confidence in the beginning. They're playful and love to wrestle, often enjoying the dance as much as the actual act of sex. Physically, *Tigers* are often fuzzy and cuddly with warm bodies.

On the other hand, *Tigers* can become fiercely jealous. For all their raw power, they tend to be transparent with their emotions and fragile when it comes to matters of the heart. When rejected, their hearts can shatter like porcelain. *Tigers* find it inconceivable that the object of their desire might not adore them and could choose someone else. Although people are easily attracted to *Tigers* at first, over time they can feel repelled by a *Tiger's* over-confidence and self-centeredness.

As new attractions arise, *Tigers* can get their loyalties confused. At these times, they often wander in the exploration of their love interests— and experience devastating ramifications. In the end, the *Tigers* feel wounded, even though they (more than likely) started the entire cascade of infidelity. Instead of seeing and accepting that, they conveniently tend to forget and dwell on their own wounded pride.

Just like the sun that's at the center of its own solar system, *Tigers* can become blinded by their own bright light.

Tiger's Higher Octave

Tigers tend to be naturally playful and loving. At core, they often believe they are at the center of the universe. The invitation for the evolving Tiger is to learn to become more sensitive to what others are actually feeling and to be less focused on themselves.

By simply shifting their awareness to how others are feeling, *Tigers* may find that new possibilities begin to emerge.

You may be pleasantly surprised by how differently others begin to treat you. Letting go of your strong beliefs and ingrained concepts can initiate powerful explorations that help you evolve to a higher octave. *Tigers* are born with powerful and, at times, overpowering natures. It's by allowing your natural exuberance to express itself fully, while at the same time tempering your focus on your own excitement and allowing others to share their contributions equally, that you will truly evolve. Perhaps by placing your gaze in this new direction and sharing the spotlight, you will find that much more becomes possible.

The Subspecies

Lion

If the *Lion* is indicated in a reading, look deeper into the qualities of leadership and social skills. Lions are far more social than all the other Big Cats and live in prides with strong family ties. Other Big Cats tend to be solitary in nature. In examining family and relationships, though, be aware that male lions tend to be lazy, letting the lionesses do most of the work, child rearing as well as hunting.

Cheetah

Cheetahs are known for their incredible speed. Not as big or powerful as the other Big Cats, they're still the fastest runners alive. However, cheetahs tire fast, and if they don't catch their prey quickly, they don't have the endurance to maintain the chase and bring it to a successful conclusion. Those with *Cheetah* qualities have a tendency to move too fast or not stay involved for the long haul. However, *Cheetahs* often have amazingly great beginnings!

Jaguars & Cougars

Jaguars and cougars are both part of the panther family. All panthers have a heightened ability to stalk and pounce with incredible stealth, moving in total silence. Unlike the cheetah, they're not fast runners so they rely on their ability to sneak up on their prey. Then, in one fluid motion, they pounce—as if coming out of nowhere. These qualities are most evident in the *Jaguar* and *Cougar* archetypes.

Aging *Cougar* women have become famous for their ability to stalk younger men, pouncing on them when they're vulnerable and can't resist—often when they're slightly inebriated. You might see aging *Cougar* women wearing Big Cat-like clothing in bars and other modern-day "watering holes." No doubt they're stalking!

Jaguars symbolize power and stealth in South America. Those with *Jaguar* qualities often are blessed with power and stealth as well as a deep knowledge of their own environment.

Black Panther

Since the 1960s, the black panther has become the symbol of power and prowess for the Black Panther Movement—a political group in the U.S. Real black panthers are truly amazing to behold; their sheer strength and incredible stealth make them the perfect symbol for reclaiming personal power.

Porcupine (Porcairian)

Porcupine: Inner and Outer Qualities

Tagline:

"Still waters run deep!"

Joke:

Two *Porcupine* women are sitting in Central Park around sunset. Two men approach and strike up a conversation with them.
Soon they separate into pairs and walk off in different directions. Both men start to make advances. The devout woman yells out, "Forgive him, Lord, for he knoweth not what he doeth!" Meanwhile, the other woman exclaims, "Too bad; mine is doing a great job!"

Porcupine Genitals:

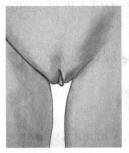 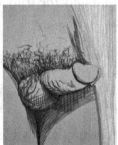

Key *Porcupine* Qualities	Shadow Side
Precise, Meticulous	Persnickety, Controlling
Clean, Practical	Perfectionistic, Harsh
Show leadership, Confident	Moody, Cunning
Smart, Independent	Fixed, Inflexible
Refined, Protective	Fussy, Fearful

Porcupines lead with their sensitive noses!

Close your eyes and imagine feeling perfectly still for a moment. Feel how your awareness can expand in all directions until it's touching the envelope of your own skin from the inside. Imagine how warm and clean this inner space feels. Feel how simple life can be, just resting inside this warm, clear inner space. The outer world feels unknown, unpredictable, and uncertain. You want to share the beauty of your warm inner space with another, but first you must be sure they are safe. You can feel how your outer skin has grown sharp cactus-like thorns to protect yourself. Your inner warm world feels precious and full of love.

Can you sense how this is your true essence? You are confident and willing to wait, knowing that only the truly worthy will be allowed to enter—and that you have so much to share.

"What a treat I have in store for you!"

Often quite attractive on the outside, *Porcupines* pay special attention to detail in how they dress and act. However, these same qualities double as a strong defense in keeping others at a distance. "Look, but don't touch!" is often the message.

Porcupine quills have long been used in creating beautiful adornments. The preferred ornamentation in many Native American tribal crafts, they're also commonly used in Africa for crafts. These quills are used to make stunning earrings and to enhance many a moccasin. But though the porcupine quills are beautiful, don't get too close or one will prick you. Ouch! Now, that really hurts!

Look into the astonishing eyes of a *Porcupine* and you'll often see a clear reflection of yourself. A *Porcupine's* eyes tend to have a crystal brilliance that reflects the universe with clarity and precision.

Porcupines tend to be careful, practical, and good with their hands. They like to keep things sparkling clean and can be methodical in their perfectionism. *Porcupines* also like having solitary time, so even when they're in a relationship, they tend to be loners. Mostly, they feel safe living in a world of their own making.

Porcupines have active, creative imaginations. In part, it's because the impenetrable "force fields" they build around themselves encourage them to create rich inner worlds.

Porcupines love justice. They're usually articulate, speak with precision and knowledge, and are masters of defensive strategies. They care about others and like to protect them, especially the young and vulnerable. They might even extend their own naturally strong defenses to help protect someone they care about. As part of their defensive strategies, *Porcupines* often pay attention to saving money and being more efficient; they're the ones who cut out coupons and research special offers.

Despite their ability to maintain perspective and be analytical, *Porcupines* have trouble making personal decisions. They tend to overanalyze and get hung up on the "what ifs." Better followers than leaders, they're most comfortable being independent.

A Native American story beautifully tells how real porcupines got their quills. Porcupines didn't always have their protective quills. In olden days, they were a desired quarry because they were so tender and tasty. They always had to run up trees to get away from predators. But because they moved slowly, they had to remain on high alert so they could get a good head start.

One day, Bear saw Porcupine and chased him up a tree, which happened to be a hawthorn tree full of thorns. Porcupine had a dreadfully painful time pulling out all the hawthorn thorns, but this gave him a brilliant idea. He chewed off an especially thorny branch and tied it to his back. The next day, Bear saw Porcupine again but instead of running for the nearest tree, Porcupine curled up in a ball exposing the hawthorn branch toward Bear. Well, as you can imagine, Bear got a paw full of thorns and ran off howling into the forest. Hugely impressed with Porcupine's ingenuity, Great Spirit immediately gifted Porcupine with amazing quills.

No matter how cold, gruff, testy, or prickly a porcupine's outside appears, know that a treasure awaits inside—just wanting to come out and play.

Porcupines in Bed

Being quite shy, *Porcupines* want to hide the scrumptious, tender beings that they are. Others often find them attractive because they tend to dress stylishly, paying attention to details such as color coordination and fashion, and making sure their clothes are clean and ironed. They often feel sexy when dressed and self-conscious when naked.

Porcupines can make stable partners, especially once their trust has been earned and outer defenses overcome. However, as loners, it's not uncommon for them to remain single or become single again later in life. Once in a partnership, though, they're not inclined to have affairs because they direct their creative juices to other pursuits, such as art, writing, sports, travel, and family. They cherish having the "space" to follow their own interests. They prefer peace and stability over the fire of passion.

Courtship outside the bedroom is an important requirement for *Porcupines*, and romance has to start way before thoughts of entering the bedroom are even on the horizon.

How do porcupines make love? Very carefully! Learning new techniques can become a preoccupation for *Porcupines*. They're drawn to learning about love positions, the art of Tantra, the Kama Sutra, and the newest edgy sexual practices. They love perfecting their skills and refining techniques, though they resist intense passion because it can feel scary and out of control for them. Despite this, they have a tendency to be vocal while making love.

Porcupines focus on cleanliness. When feeling receptive, they often invite their lover to share in a sensuous shower or bath before sex. Combining sensuality and cleanliness, they can be more sexually fun in the shower than in bed. Their "quills" get wet and lie flat against their bodies, making it easier to get close to them at these times.

Conversely, when *Porcupines* become agitated, their quills stick straight out and they can be very difficult to get close to. They might say all kinds of prickly things, especially related to one of their favorite topics, cleanliness. For example, they might point out that you smell bad, you have a filthy mind, or your clothes, house, and/or car are ungodly messes. With a million and one ways to repel you, their quills can be quite sharp.

That said, *Porcupines* can display an amazing ability to hide what they're feeling. In fact, they can be so convincing, they might actually fool themselves as well. Sometimes, they even come to believe what they're portraying.

Some *Porcupines* get a little outrageous when they're totally at ease. It's not common for any of the 12 animal totem types to engage in the Golden Showers Ritual. (Note: Golden Showers refers to urinating as part of foreplay. *Porcupines* are one of the few species that actually urinate on their mates as part of their courtship ritual.) Of all the totems, *Porcupines* are more likely than any of the others to do so (especially in the shower). The *Porcupine* is clearly relaxed when he or she invites you to share in this rare ritual.

Porcupine's Higher Octave

Porcupines tend to be careful and cautious by nature. At core, they are very protective and put up formable defensive exteriors, finding themselves often alone yet quite content. The invitation for the evolving *Porcupine* is to learn through their own life experience to open and gradually allow others in.

Simply by being more trusting, you will find that new possibilities start to emerge. You may be pleasantly surprised by what begins to happen. Letting go of your judgments and concepts can initiate powerful explorations that help you evolve to a higher octave. *Porcupines* are born with tender natures. Perhaps it's by allowing your natural protectiveness to express itself fully, while at the same time taking new risks and opening to others, that you will truly evolve. Allow your heart to be soft and feel how the gentle ebb and flow of life's journey can seduce you.

Dolphin (Dolphinfish)

Dolphin (Dolphinian)

Dolphin: Primary Qualities

Tagline:

"Let's play!"

Joke:

"If I were to tell you that you have a beautiful body,
would you hold it against me?"

Dolphin Genitals:

Key *Dolphin* Qualities	Shadow Side
Loving, Romantic	Persnickety, Controlling
Diplomatic, Social	Gullible, Shallow
Easy-going, Peaceful	Latently angry, Indifferent
Positive, Charming	Changeable, Indecisive
Fair, Playful	Too Self-sacrificing, Indignant

Dolphins lead with their skin. And at times with their laughter!

Imagine you are happy—so happy you feel like leaping into the air as high as you can. Feel how your feet whoosh into the air as the rest of your body tumbles forward. Can you feel how your arms and legs want to extend outward like a starfish's? Before you know what's happening, your body is cartwheeling for the pure pleasure of it!

Feelings of joy arise and you smile open-heartedly. Your body feels amazingly strong and full of life. You feel like you could do anything, travel anywhere. You sense others moving toward you now. Can you feel how your tribe is circling around you? They're singing in unison. A profound feeling of harmony overcomes you.

Can you feel how you're one with all of existence—that there's no separation—swimming, playing, singing, and living in this watery oceanic community?

"Now, let's really play!"

Dolphins are often physically beautiful. They worship beauty and love to be surrounded by it. Drawn to the natural, they tend to be unconcerned with adornment but are attracted to sparkly jewelry. Rarely focused on clothing or make-up they often have naturally luminous skin. They are captivated especially by beautiful hair.

The pink Boto dolphins found in the Amazon River are believed to be shape shifters, capable of having children with human women. The indigenous people of the Amazon River basin won't kill and eat the Boto because they believe these dolphins used to be human long ago and some believe they can become human again at will. They say that the Boto shape shift into handsome young men at night and seduce their women, impregnating them before returning to the river in the morning and becoming dolphins once again.

Dolphin people tend to be just as sensuous as the Boto and live fully in their bodies. Because they thrive in both the air and the water, they have the ability to move between worlds and even embrace mystical qualities.

As social creatures, *Dolphins* love to communicate. They're extremely intelligent but tend not to be highly intellectual. They can bond deeply in many different ways and thrive on a kind of psychic, mystical connection that transcends both mind and emotions. You might see them dancing, touching, singing, laughing.

When dolphin mammals get excited, their white underbellies turn pink. Similarly, *Dolphins* tend to be transparent and show their emotions easily.

Dolphins naturally gravitate toward peace and seek balance while navigating the turbulent oceans of emotion. Less concerned with right and wrong, they prefer to maintain equanimity. Their shadow side of anger can flair up surprisingly quickly if they believe they're entangled in a downward spiraling dynamic. But the anger often passes as quickly as clouds pass over the sun.

In Greek mythology, the god Dionysus was captured by pirates who believed he was a wealthy prince they could ransom. When the pirate ship was far out to sea, Dionysus called on his supernatural powers to conjure up vines that covered the ship, mast, and sails. As his anger grew, he changed the oars into serpents so terrifying that the sailors jumped overboard. But Dionysus took pity on the pirate sailors and transformed them into dolphins so they could spend their lives giving help to those in need. Thereafter, dolphins were believed to be the messengers of Poseidon, the Greek god of the sea.

Full of heart, *Dolphins* often help others raise their energy levels and coax the less fortunate out of depression. Their contagiously playful nature can inspire others. Their singing is haunting. As great communicators, they seem to commune on many levels.

If you have been fortunate enough to swim with dolphins, you might have looked into a dolphin's eyes and felt its beatific smile. This experience will likely live with you for the rest of your life—as it will when you interact with human *Dolphins*.

Dolphins in Bed

Closely aligned with the planet Venus, *Dolphins* are natural lovers—a quality that guides many of their life choices.

Dolphins are the only other mammals besides humans who make love for the pure joy of it, not just for procreation. Like their totem animal, *Dolphins* love to dance, frolic, and explore multitudes of different positions in which to make love. Because they love to play sexually for fun, *Dolphins* sometimes appear promiscuous to others.

Also like their totem, *Dolphins* are incredibly sensitive to and aware of where they reside in space, both physically and emotionally. In the sea, dolphins use a sophisticated system of sending out sounds and listening for echoes, much like sonar. This allows them to be extremely attuned to their environment. Human *Dolphins* use a similar strategy when navigating through life. Sensitive to and aware of other people's feelings, they can digest huge amounts of subtle information quickly, an ability most other totems don't possess. Using their psychic sonar to attune to others, they navigate through the emotional waters of life with precision and grace.

Dolphins are intuitive, and even though they're highly intelligent, they often choose to express their passion for life non verbally. They love full-body contact and hugging, often initiating playful games that call for loving touch. Comfortable with eye contact, *Dolphins* can sink deeply into the experience. Often wonderful dancers, their playful spirits are contagious.

Dolphins are good with their hands and love sensuous massage. Because they don't have much patience for lovers who tend to be serious, they often avoid interacting with the serious personality types.

Dolphins are comfortable inside themselves as well as in the world at large. They are happy just floating and relaxing in this ocean of life. *Nowhere to go, nothing to do, just being; here for the grace of love go I.*

Dolphin's Higher Octave

Dolphins are playful and loving by nature. At core, they exude a grace and lightness of being that is a joy to experience. At times *Dolphins* may appear to be superficial, lacking in commitment and depth. The invitation for evolving *Dolphins* is to learn to become more patient with the entanglements that other humans often find themselves in.

By simply shifting their awareness to sympathize with how others are feeling, *Dolphins* may find that new possibilities begin to emerge.

You may be pleasantly surprised by how differently others begin to treat you as they sense that you truly care. Letting go of your strong need to feel unencumbered can initiate a powerful exploration that helps you evolve to a higher octave. *Dolphins* are born as free spirits. It's by allowing your natural desire to be free to express itself fully, while at the same time exploring how you can grow to become more committed, that you will truly evolve. Selfless service often leads to a wonderful higher octave for *Dolphins* to explore.

Snake (Snakes)

Snake: Primary Qualities

Tagline:

"Come here; I won't bite you."

Joke:

"What is the sexiest snake?"
"The bushmaster!"

Snake Genitals:

Key *Snake* Qualities	Shadow Side
Magnetic, Powerful	Mesmerizing, Obsessive
Passionate, Determined	Jealous, Controlling
Unwavering, Confident	Inflexible, Obstinate
Intuitive, Emotional	Resentful, Guarded
Intelligent, Mysterious	Compulsive, Secretive

Snakes lead with their eyes!

Can you feel your own power and magnetism emanating from every cell in your body? Imagine how your captivating beauty and intelligence affect others. Feel how your core strength is circling, coiling, in your belly. Your mind, lit up like a city at night, complex yet synchronized.

Can you feel that quiet explosion now growing in your genitals?

Allowing your strong animal magnetism to radiate, can you feel how others are drawing nearer to you?

"Yes! Come closer; I won't bite you."

Snakes tend to have cool personalities, appearing to be unemotional. Yet, at the same time, they're often subtly magnetic and can have a hypnotic effect on others. They prefer to remain on an even keel so their piercing, ancient eyes and keen intelligence can fully take in their total surroundings. All the while, under their apparent indifference, a host of emotions could well be seething. *Snakes* are extremely emotional but they rarely let others see this aspect of their being—it's part of their survival strategy.

Drawn to power, *Snakes* strive to win. Fearless, they have an innate understanding of the mysteries of life and death. When betrayed, they can become intensely vindictive, often dealing out double doses of the venom they perceive was dealt to them. On the other hand, when treated with generosity, *Snakes* can be equally magnanimous, double dosing their benefactor in kind. Above all else, *Snakes* prize loyalty.

Tending to move with an inner grace not common to the other animal totems, *Snakes* are extremely flexible and surprisingly strong physically.

Real snakes have a primal energy that holds the power of life and death. Poisonous snakes contain venom that's often deadly—yet this same venom can be milked and transformed into life-giving anti-venom. *Snakes* possess this same double-edged sword.

When snakes shed their skins, an interesting phenomenon occurs. Their eyes cloud over and, for a brief moment, they become blind, but the actual skin (cornea) covering their eyes does not shed. Look closely at a shed snakeskin and you will see holes in the skin where the eyes were once located. When a snake grows its new skin, the eyes alone remain unchanged.

A snake shedding its skin provides an intriguing metaphor for the process of reincarnation. The soul sheds its personality and dons a new one during each cycle of death and rebirth. It could be said that snake eyes, unchanged, are like the eternal soul that remains unchanged throughout the many lives and personalities into which it reincarnates. It could even be said that the snake's moment of blindness is akin to the soul's transition between death and rebirth.

Like the eternal soul, *Snake* eyes are truly ancient.

Thus, it's not surprising to find that *Snake* eyes often have a piercing, ancient quality. *Snakes* know the secret of metamorphosis through their own soul's journey and are often old souls residing in new bodies. Their ancient eyes usually give them away. They're frequently drawn to artifacts and often become obsessed, delving into old mysteries and ancient secrets. It's almost as if they're searching for lost knowledge or memories from earlier incarnations.

Snakes love to make eye contact and often engage until the other person turns away—a sure-fire way to know that you've encountered a

Snake. Despite their intensity, *Snakes*—not wanting to give away what they know or feel—often present facial expressions that remain cool and even-tempered. *Snakes* need to know the particulars of everything going on around them, yet rarely do they show their own hand. They believe that secrecy gives them great power.

Snakes are perhaps the most misunderstood of all the animal totems. They are usually looked upon with fear, although not in every culture. *Snakes* represent ancient souls with a deep understanding of both life and death. The image of a snake biting its own tail is the most ancient and prized symbol of all time—The Ouroboros, the circle of life and death. The Ouroboros represents the perpetual cyclic renewal of life leading to immortality.

In the East, serpent images are often accepted as part of the whole of existence. The image of Kali, the goddess of death, includes snakes. As the face of the circle of life, death, and rebirth, she represents the great balance between life and death.

In the West and in Judeo-Christian tradition, however, snakes aren't regarded favorably. In the Old Testament story of the Garden of Eden, the serpent's role in man's fall from the grace of God has greatly influenced Western culture and thinking. In certain Christian sects, people handle vipers with their bare hands as part of a ceremony that tests the depth of their personal faith.

This foundational myth concerning snakes has been detrimental to the image of women over time. In the Biblical story of Adam and Eve, Eve convinces Adam to disobey God and eat from the Tree of the Knowledge of Good and Evil. But the snake caused Eve to persuade Adam to eat the apple, thereby introducing original sin. Influenced in part by the snake's phallic shape, people have been led to believe that sex is somehow connected to evil.

Knowledge of good and evil—the basis of both sin and shame—ruined Adam and Eve's innocent bliss. They became aware of their nakedness only after eating an apple from the Tree of Knowledge and felt shame for the first time. And, as the story goes, they immediately covered their genitals with fig leaves.

Ultimately, God throws Adam and Eve out of the Garden of Eden (a metaphor for the bliss of innocence that preceded the knowledge of good and evil). From then on, sex has been associated with humanity's fall from the grace of God.

In contrast, many other cultures view snakes as powerful creators and teachers of renewal. Even one of the American culture's most familiar icons, the symbol of the American Medical Association (AMA), shows two snakes coiled around the staff of life. The symbol represents healing, life, and renewal.

Snakes in Bed

Snakes have the ability to transmit their sexual shakti on an energetic level. Often, intended recipients can feel their own genitals responding the moment they meet the *Snake's* penetrating gaze.

Have you ever examined snakes carefully to see where their genitals are? Hard to find? That's because the entire snake is often seen as one giant phallic symbol!

Of all the totem types, *Snakes* have the most sexually intense personas. They're extremely passionate, frequently have magnetic personalities, and radiate strong sexual energy. Often, they gaze with such intensity that one feels naked even when fully dressed. Their magnetism is, at times, hypnotic. They love connecting physically, but even more, they revel in imbuing their lovemaking with mystical and euphoric qualities.

Snakes deeply bond with their lovers. They rarely tiptoe about; rather, they jump into love with their whole being. Highly sensitive, *Snakes* feel deeply and are frequently self-absorbed. When they're positively oriented, they can become inspiring lovers. But when they're overcome by negativity, they can turn toward the dark side. At these times, they become intensely jealous and hold resentments for years. More than any other totem, when consumed by their shadow side, *Snakes* can become ruthless—almost sinister—in their meticulously planned strategies of revenge and dominance. Like a rattlesnake, they know how to wait patiently, striking their deadly blow at just the right moment.

Fortunately, however, *Snakes* usually stay connected to their higher selves. Because they're also extremely intelligent, they tend to use their sexual magnetism to attract healthy situations that allow for deep, meaningful connections.

Watch a snake for a while. You'll see how amazingly flexible their bodies are, yet strong and powerful at the same time. *Snakes* have between 100 and 400 vertebrae with ribs attached to each one of them. Snake totem types often share these qualities. They enjoy taking care of their bodies and have strong yet supple physiques. They love to arch and stretch, often working out in some fashion. As a result, they can become highly creative in mastering a wide variety of different lovemaking positions.

Often *Snakes* find their deepest connection in stillness, and through connecting in stillness with their lover, their orgasms can reach mind-blowing heights. They despise mechanical lovers who have preplanned, learned techniques. Indeed, *Snakes* get turned off if they have the slightest inkling that their lover wants to manipulate them in any way, even if their lover's intentions are pure at heart. They require their lovers to be present and original.

Snakes are often drawn to yoga and excel at mastering postures. Preferring to be in control, they're highly rebellious. For this reason, they often feel alone and, even in partnership, remain highly independent. Although on the physical level, they can merge deeply and with great passion with their lovers, *Snakes* often reserve their thoughts and aspirations for themselves alone.

Snake's Higher Octave

Snakes tend, by nature, to be intense and strategic. At core, they love to be secretive and to strive for control. The invitation for the evolving *Snake* is to learn through their own life experience to soften and to be more transparent about their own feelings. Perhaps by relaxing their need for control and power, *Snakes* will find that new possibilities begin to arise. Rich inner experiences, not connected to sovereignty over others, may begin to emerge and can develop into a direct connection with God.

By shifting your gaze to a more relaxed vantage point as an evolved *Snake*, you can retain your natural ability to hold power, yet at the same time, soften and become more vulnerable. You may be pleasantly surprised by what you find. In this way you will begin to experience a higher octave of the *Snake* archetype. It's by allowing your own natural intensity to express itself fully, while at the same time remaining soft and receptive, that new possibilities truly emerge. Just like water, *Snakes* can have diverse qualities. Water is hard on impact when you dive in from high above, yet soft and flowing when you are immersed in its flow. Its softness carves rocks and it always flows downward, never trying to rise above; yet nothing is more powerful than water. Consider becoming the water *Snake*.

The Subspecies

Boa Snake

When the *Boa* is evident, it indicates these *Snakes* are inclined to smother and overpower their lovers.

Rattle Snake

When the *Rattlesnake* is evident, they tend to strike out with intensity toward their lovers.

King Snake

When the *King Snake* shows up, they're inclined to pretend to be dangerous but in actuality are caring and dependable. They tend to champion the world with their power to overcome dangerous and dark forces. Think of a scary-looking, tattooed, Hells Angel biker who's kindhearted and rides his bike with the spirit of a knight from King Arthur's roundtable— righting wrongs and fighting injustices in the world.

Coral Snake

Look carefully, though, because he may be a deadly *Coral Snake* and not the *King Snake* you first thought. Appearances can be deceiving so be sure to use your discretion.

Frog/Toad (Frogarian)

Frog/Toad: Primary Qualities

Tagline:

"Kiss me! I'm really a prince/princess!"

Joke:

"What did one frog say to another?"
"Time is fun when you're having flies!"

Frog/Toad Genitals:

 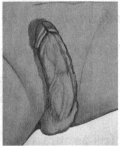

Key *Frog* Qualities	Shadow Side
Free-spirited, Optimistic	Naïve, Careless
Jovial, Happy-go-lucky	Superficial, Irresponsible
Simple, Honest	Gullible, Tactless
Intellectual, Philosophical	Heady, Dwells on the Past
Ubiquitous, Able to flow	Restless, Indecisive
Travel-loving, Heart-full	Frustrated with details

Frogs lead with their spirituality!

Imagine you're squatting on your favorite lily pad basking in the late afternoon sun, happily awaiting nightfall. A riotous choir of croaking and singing arises from the shoreline. You take in a deep breath, filling your lungs to capacity. With one big croak, you open your mouth as wide as wide can be, singing your heart-song into the open night sky.

Soon you find yourself hopping from lily pad to lily pad, searching for the source of that illusive song you just heard across the pond—the song of your beloved. You follow the melody until you arrive at last in the welcoming webbed arms that await you.

"Kiss me! I'm really a prince/princess!"

Frogs often don't feel as attractive as they would like themselves to be. Fortunately, their rich inner worlds keep them from focusing on such external and trivial concerns. The key to understanding frog energy is metamorphosis. More than any other totem, *Frogs* can morph before your eyes. At times, they may appear harsh and a bit brash, but then they can quickly transform themselves into appearing light-hearted and funny. Often, the closer you get, the more beautiful they appear.

Real frogs and toads live in two worlds—that of water and that of air. In addition, certain species of toads (Bufo) have an extremely powerful psychedelic agent in their skins called bufotenin. In their healing rituals, Native American shamans used this toad venom to journey between this world and other dimensions. The smallest amount of this powerful psychedelic can completely transform one's perception of reality; take the slightest bit too much and you cross over (die).

Frogs embody this same ability to live in multiple worlds. As natural masters of inter-dimensional travel, they understand the journey of metamorphosis (from pollywog to frog) from their own soul's journey. They can help others experience the same.

Usually positive and upbeat in their attitude toward life, *Frogs* can be quite jovial. They have deep reserves and often remain optimistic even when surrounded by pessimistic personalities. They choose to live life simply and in the present.

Compelled to tell the truth, *Frogs* may be quite tactless in their delivery of this truth. In their own minds, they're just being frank and mean no harm. They might even add a touch of wry humor. But despite the *Frog's* lack of malice, the recipient may well feel emotionally attacked and get upset. And, in trying to remedy the situation—once they realize that they've offended someone—*Frogs* usually end up digging themselves deeper into a hole.

Frogs tend to have fantastic memories. It can be uncanny how they remember the exact date that something occurred 27 years ago. They even remember such details as the color of the socks someone was wearing at the time. On the other hand, they can be incredibly absent-minded when it comes to the practical, physical realm—like leaving their wallets somewhere, losing their car keys, or not realizing their glasses they've been searching for during the past half hour have been neatly perched on their heads the whole time.

Often attracted to speed, *Frogs* usually love to drive fast (if they can remember where they put their car keys!). In addition, they tend to be fearless and enjoy taking risks. Drawn to gambling at times, they're often willing to gamble in all matters of life, including love and money.

On their shadow side, *Frogs* can display explosive anger, especially if they feel misunderstood or unjustly accused. At these times, they can be verbally abusive and, if agitated enough, could strike out physically. Usually by the next day, all is forgiven. *Frogs* don't tend to hold grudges.

Because *Frogs* like to travel, they're often attracted to careers that take them to exotic countries. They constantly explore new places in their physical as well as internal worlds.

Idealistic and drawn to championing injustices, *Frogs* can often be found supporting various fringe groups and associations. Although basically independent, they tend to be comfortable in large crowds.

Lovers of animals, *Frog* people often have pets. At the very least, they're the first to pet another's dog. They can be quite accomplished at petting!

Frogs are frequently found in European myths and fairytales. Two well-known expressions are both classic lines from the fairytale *The Frog Prince*, representing flip sides of the same ancient archetype: "Kiss me! I'm really a prince (princess)!" and "You have to kiss a lot of frogs before you find your prince (princess)." Almost every woman knows both of these lines!

In the story *The Frog Prince*, a witch turns a handsome prince into a frog. She tells him he'll be released from her curse only if he can find a princess who recognizes him for who he truly is and kisses him. Once the kiss of true love occurs, the frog magically transforms back into the prince. A true metamorphosis!

This parallels the conditions of a frog's metamorphosis and the journey from pollywog, or tadpole, to frog. Pollywogs actually have gills. During their metamorphosis into mature frogs, they lose their gills and grow lungs so they can breathe air. Not just *any* lungs, but amazingly powerful lungs. Images of the famous trumpet player Louis Armstrong come to mind—huge, puffed-out cheeks hitting a sustained high note while smiling at the same time, then singing in his raspy frog-like voice with joy and candor. Have you ever observed bullfrogs croaking? They swell up like a balloon, sucking in a huge amount of air in order to sing out a celebration of their very existence.

In Japan, frogs are often considered symbols of good luck. One myth says all bullfrogs originally descended from a great ancestor who could suck all the mosquitoes out of a whole room in a single breath. Now, can life get any better than that?

Frogs/Toads in Bed

Frogs are less concerned with physical prowess than with mystical qualities. They tend to have sparkling Jupiter eyes reflecting their deep inner nature. Because *Frogs* have rich inner worlds, beautiful princesses and princes are drawn to their ability to open magical new worlds.

Likewise, *Frogs* are less concerned with the physical qualities of lovemaking, being more drawn to the spiritual qualities of love. Often they have exceptionally beautiful lovers because of the deep spiritual connection they emanate. *Beauty is often drawn to spiritual depth because she feels "seen" for her true self, not just her outer beauty.*

Frogs can be a bit narcissistic. Real frogs shed their skins four times a year and then immediately eat them. In their own eyes, *Frogs* see themselves as beautiful and at the center of the universe. They can be demanding and, at the same time, easy going. Usually simple and direct, they prefer things that way, even if they have difficulty living up to their own expectations. They tend to be straightforward in bed.

Real frogs are symbols for fertility and harbingers of rain for many cultures. After a summer rain, one can sometimes find thousands of newly hatched baby frogs hopping around a body of water.

In ancient Egypt, the banks of the Nile River would become so overrun with frogs during mating season that frogs, creation, and birth became linked in the Egyptian mind. Specifically, they became associated with the goddess Heqet (or Heket), who was the goddess of fertility and childbirth. Heqet was often portrayed as a frog-woman with a frog's head and a woman's body. She was the protector for childbirth, and midwives often wore an amulet with her image on it.

Frogs tend to have large extended families but don't always have children themselves. Family is a priority for them, although *Frogs* can easily become workaholics and spend long periods away from their partners and families. They're naturally loyal partners, but if rejected, they can fall into a reactive spiral and enter a long phase of promiscuity.

More than any other totem, *Frogs* create deeply emotional yet often asexual connections with friends and business associates. At times, this can confuse their partners who could feel rejected even though these relationships are not sexual in nature.

Just like real frogs, *Frogs* love to croak and groan, often being verbally loud in bed. Usually nocturnal, they often rally their sexual energies after the sun goes down. Their favorite time of day is twilight when they find themselves sliding into the shifting light. They know full well that magic lives and possibilities abound.

Frog's Higher Octave

Frogs tend to be mystical and playful by nature. At core, they're happy and exude confidence. The invitation for the evolving *Frog* is to learn to pay more attention to the everyday physical world, thereby bringing balance to an innately rich inner world. *Frogs* can be a bit narcissistic; as they move towards a higher octave of their archetype, they begin to place their attention more on others and listen on a deeper level. Perhaps that is why we were given 2 ears and only one mouth. *Frogs* often have wonderful mouths, but for the evolving *Frog*, it's the ears that require opening.

By simply shifting your awareness more towards others and truly listening to how they feel, you will likely find that new possibilities begin to emerge.

You may be pleasantly surprised by how differently others begin to treat you. Letting go of your strong beliefs and quick-flare-up brand of anger, can initiate powerful explorations that will help you evolve to a higher octave. Perhaps it's by allowing your natural exuberance to express itself fully, while at the same time tempering your focus on your own excitement and allowing others to equally share their contributions, that you will truly evolve. The deeper you can listen, the more you will receive that which you most cherish!

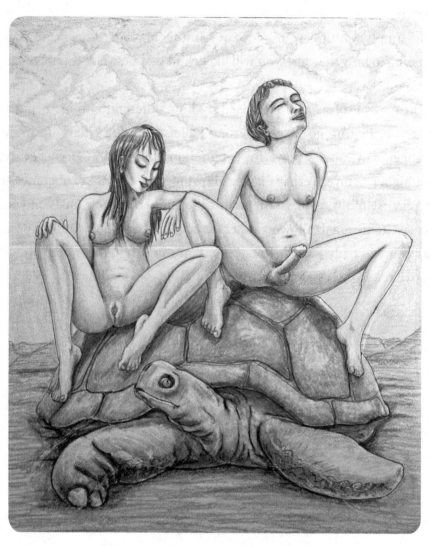

Turtle/Tortoise (Terrapin)

Turtle/Tortoise: Primary Qualities

Tagline:

"Step by step . . . I am victorious!"

Joke:

A rather upset *Turtle* describes to a police officer how he was robbed and attacked by a gang of slugs. The officer says, "Calm down and tell me what happened." The *Turtle* replies, "I don't know! Everything happened so fast!"

Turtle/Tortoise Genitals:

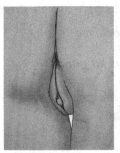 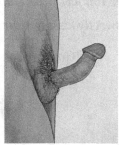

Key *Turtle* Qualities	Shadow Side
Practical, Patient	Pessimistic, Docile
Humorous, Prudent	Slow, Miserly
Careful, Disciplined	Rigid, Fearful
Self-contained, Reserved	Fatalistic, Resentful
Ambitious	Overly competitive

Turtles lead with their self-reliance!

Imagine sitting on a rock at midday, the fall sun pleasantly warming your body. Not too hot, not too cold. You feel perfect!

Time passes and you're melting into the stone, absorbing all the warmth of the day into the cells of your body. Overcome with fatigue, your eyelids feel heavy now, but you want to open them anyway. With a little effort, you crack them open ever so slightly. Through squinting eyes, you can see that the sun has arced farther down its trajectory while you were sleeping. Lo and behold, your partner has quietly climbed up on your rock to catch the last rays of sunshine by your side. You smile. Then you notice something stirring inside you. You feel warm and tingly as you stretch your neck out to rub foreheads, sweetly kissing your beloved.

"Going slow is so good."

Turtles have an ancient quality about them. They're old souls, something you can sense in their eyes even if they're young in years. They move through space with care and intention. They exude wisdom; they love to learn and are eager to understand how things work.

Turtles are usually prepared for any occasion. When traveling, they enjoy camper-type vehicles so they can carry their homes around with them, on wheels. At these times, they are totally in their element.

Attracted to browns, blacks, muted greens, and gold, *Turtles* tend to wear earth-colored clothing. They feel comfortable on land as well as in water and love spending time where they can access both, especially where they can intermittently bask in the sun and cool off in the water. Rarely do they get bored; they enjoy moving slowly and relaxing in familiar spaces.

Exceedingly practical and steady, *Turtles* are reliable and usually follow through on most of the projects they begin. Competitive by nature, they often succeed through fortitude and sheer perseverance.

They can also slip into circular thinking and ruminate on negative thoughts, spiraling into resentful, petty, and fearful realms. When *Turtles* get caught in this kind of thinking, they can become quite fixated and hard to shift.

Real turtles can actually feel touch through their protective shells because a complex network of sensitive nerve endings extends throughout their shells. Likewise, although *Turtles* don't appear to be affected by emotional circumstances, they're acutely aware of what's going on. They're carefully processing incoming data—slowly. With inexhaustible patience, they can outlast just about any adversary.

Turtles are well described in Aesop's famous fable *The Tortoise and the Hare*. In this tale, the hare (rabbit) taunts a tortoise about being so slow moving. The tortoise immediately challenges the hare to a race. Of course, the fast rabbit runs far ahead of the tortoise in the beginning, but being overconfident, stops to take a leisurely nap. Meanwhile, the tortoise plods slowly but steadily along, soon passing the sleeping rabbit. He finishes first!

A friend once asked if I knew why turtles live so long. The oldest tortoise ever documented was Tu'I Malila, a present to the Tongan royal family from the famed British explorer Captain Cook. Tu'I Malila died of natural causes in 1965 at the ripe old age of 188.

When I said I didn't know, she told me, "I have watched sea turtles carefully. They chew their food incredibly slowly with their total presence focused on each chew. It's as if there was absolutely nothing else in the world happening."

Turtles digest everything in life slowly, with presence and awareness, and they tend to live a long time due to their calm natures.

Turtle/Tortoise in Bed

Turtles tend to be steady and long-lasting lovers. Generally even-keeled, they're less emotional than many other animal totem types. Although they can become jealous, the issue more often centers on control rather than sexual passion.

While adept at the mechanics of love, *Turtles* prefer that others supply the emotions and electricity. They love to study and acquire knowledge; they're often attracted to books and workshops that teach techniques, positions, and skill sets that help them be masterful lovers on the physical level. Normally very patient, they love to go slowly. *Turtle* males can make love for a long time without ejaculating. They enjoy staying in control and are often drawn to disciplines such as Tantra, which discourage emotion as a motivating force.

Turtles aren't usually motivated by originality either; they rely on classic traditions they can study and learn from. Indeed, they can spend countless hours, days, weeks, and even years becoming proficient. They're driven to be the best at whatever they set their minds to accomplish.

Turtles tend to be self-contained and can be less social than many other totem types. When they do connect intimately, they often become life partners. Although they likely have only a few friends, they value these friendships deeply and remain loyal for life.

Turtles have a tendency to be pessimistic, naturally dwelling on what can go wrong. When they feel emotionally uncomfortable, they conveniently slip back into their protective shells and wait for a better time to come out. After a while, they tentatively stick their heads out again and look around to see what's happening. *Turtles* know there's plenty of time for everything!

Turtle's Higher Octave

Turtles tend to be cautious and self-contained by nature. At core, they are very protective and develop formable defensive exteriors, often finding themselves alone even when in partnership. The invitation is for the evolving *Turtle* to learn through their own life experience to open more and gradually allow others in. Positive thinking may become a life-long mode of exploration.

By simply being more trusting and shifting to positive thoughts, new possibilities start to emerge.

You may be pleasantly surprised by what begins to happen. Letting go of your judgments and concepts can initiate powerful discoveries that help you evolve to a higher octave. *Turtles* are born with sensitive natures. It's by allowing your natural protectiveness to express itself fully, while at the same time taking new risks and opening your inner being to positive thoughts, that you will truly evolve. Thick shells can be wonderfully protective and can act like guardians for the semi-porous or open mind, but all too often protective shells turn into closed minded guards that become rigid and harsh. Guard or guardian, —the choice is always yours.

Pheasant/Peacock (Peacoshians)

Pheasant/Peacock: Primary Qualities

Tagline:

"I am beautiful! Look at me!"

Joke:

"How many *Peacocks* does it take to change a light bulb?"
"None. I am the light show!"

Peacock Genitals:

 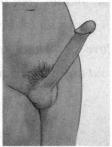

Key *Pheasant/Peacock* Qualities	Shadow Side
Physically Beautiful, Friendly	Prideful, Stubborn
Original, Inventive	Unpredictable, Perverse
Free-spirited, Intellectual	Unemotional, Detached
Humanitarian, Tolerant	Dogmatic, Willful
Honest, Loyal	Condescending, Idealistic

Peacocks lead with their hair!

Imagine flying high above the earth, tracing the arc of a rainbow. As if in a dream, you can feel the different colors stretch out before you. You enjoy this sensation of rising above the mundane activities of everyday life. Your lover quietly sleeps beside you, looking beautiful, dreaming peacefully.

Your attention shifts, and you're looking into the future now. You can clearly see where the rainbow you're traveling on arcs back to the earth and touches the ground.

You're a visionary, and for you, this rainbow represents the real world. You'd rather live in the world of dreams and visions than anywhere else. You can feel your love for all humanity, for everyone. Truly, it feels almost belittling to single out any one person to be the object of love.

"Why limit love?"

Peacocks embody a striving toward beauty, truth, and perfection here on earth. They enjoy groups and often talk of brotherhood, sisterhood, and everyone being a friend. Seekers of the truth, they're usually open-minded and willing to consider many different points of view.

However, when they're shut down emotionally, they can become the exact opposite; they become dogmatic and unable to hear any opinions but their own. At these times, they can even slip into feeling betrayed and become angry. *Peacocks* have been known to have a terrible shriek-bark and can be quite intimidating when they use it. Luckily, most of the time they're good tempered and friendly.

Peacocks usually have keen minds and enjoy the endless dissection of human dynamics. Inquisitive by nature, they're often ready to ask astute questions. At other times, they can seem distracted and distant, appearing not to care in the least. Sometimes they appear to look out of dreamy eyes, as if they're seeing into some kind of possible future. It's hardly surprising that their diverse range of personality traits can be confusing to their friends and lovers.

In ancient China, the peacock represented beauty, power, and divinity. In fact, it was believed that a woman could get pregnant merely by exchanging glances with a peacock!

Just as the peacock is adorned with a myriad of beautiful colors, *Peacocks* are attracted to everything related to rainbows. They love that multiple-colored rainbows bridge this world with the magic of the future's infinite possibilities. *Peacocks* are strongly influenced by the planet Uranus, which means they are farseeing and have a unique vantage point.

Peacocks have the wonderful ability to see the many sides of any argument, embodying the power of the all-seeing eye motif. Perhaps this comes from their peacock totem whose tail feathers possess hundreds of eyes. With so many eyes, *Peacocks* can see clearly—in the realm of here and now, and into the future as well.

Pheasants/Peacocks in Bed

As part of the *Pheasant* family, *Peacocks* have a wide variety of attributes, but all seem to have a deeper affinity for the love of all humankind than for the personal intimacy of one on one.

Peacocks tend to be quite surprising. Have you ever startled a pheasant while peacefully walking through the woods? It suddenly shoots up into the sky releasing loud cries with a fluttering of feathers. Well, reflecting the noisy behavior of a typical pheasant, when *Peacocks* have an orgasm, the whole neighborhood knows about it. They tend to enjoy sharing their experiences with everyone! And then again, they may just as likely be completely silent.

Two distinct personas can appear with *Peacocks* in bed. Some are demure, with muted colors and shy personalities mirroring female peahens. Others are extroverted, often with brilliant colors and loud characteristics mirroring male peacocks. Note: These characteristics aren't gender specific for *Peacock* archetypes. A wide variety of both personality types appear in both genders.

Peacocks of the showier variety border on being exhibitionists. They love to wear brilliant-colored clothing and adorn themselves with sparkling jewelry. They can be attractive in an over-the-top kind of way. Although they love to be seen, they often have difficulty developing deep personal relationships. *Peacocks* can appear superficial, but in actuality, they possess considerable depth and sensitivity.

Peacock women may have breast augmentation surgery and *Peacock* men may have hair implants. Looking good is highly important to a *Peacock*. Being quite open, *Peacocks* can flow with others. They love the unexpected and are often versatile in their talents.

Whether they have quiet or extroverted personalities, *Peacocks* tend to be fiercely independent. Above all else, they love the truth and always seek it, looking into the future to explore what's possible.

Peacocks can be standoffish at first; to some, they might appear aloof and unapproachable. Although they often have a "look but do not touch" persona, once they believe you are truthful—their yardstick for worthiness—they become more affectionate and will allow you in.

Often *Peacocks* develop into tenacious friends and lovers, ready to sacrifice everything for their partners. But just as easily, they can remain solitary and prefer feeling free and independent. Clearly, the spectrum of *Peacock* attributes and sub-types is diverse, which can be both confusing and surprising for their intimates. Word of advice: Never betray *Peacocks*; their anger can be extreme. Paradoxically, after a rather unpleasant breakup, they're likely to say, "Can't we still be friends?"

Peacock's Higher Octave

Peacocks tend to be outwardly oriented and are drawn to surface qualities. At core, they are visionaries, filled with love for all humanity and tending to shy away from romantic love. At times *Peacocks* may appear to be superficial and may seem to lack the ability to be intimate on a personal level. The invitation for the evolving *Peacock* is to look deeper into the present moment rather than fantasizing about an idealized future, and to become more vulnerable and more receptive to one-on-one intimacy.

Simply by shifting your gaze to the here and now, you will find that new possibilities begin to emerge.

You may be pleasantly surprised by how differently others treat you when they find that you are truly open to connecting on a personal level. Letting go of your strong need to feel unencumbered can initiate a powerful exploration that will help you evolve to a higher octave. *Peacocks* are born as free spirits. Perhaps it's by allowing your aloof and visionary nature to express itself fully, while at the same time exploring ways to become more vulnerable and present, that you will truly evolve... *resting in knowing that—truth takes time!*

Seahorse (Sea-airian)

Seahorse: Primary Qualities

Tagline:

"Let the magic ever be."

Joke:

"When seahorses get sick, what kind of doctor do they go to?"
"A sturgeon!"

Seahorse Genitals:

Key *Seahorse* Qualities	Shadow Side
Selfless, Intuitive	Idealistic, Gullible
Kind, Compassionate	Weak willed, Naïve
Imaginative, Creative	Vague, Idealistic
Sensitive, Caring	Secretive, Escapist
Spiritual, Non-materialistic	Unrealistic, Low-achieving

Seahorses lead with their auras, with their ability to attune!

Imagine the sun slipping below the brilliant horizon and the magical twilight infusing your essence with its golden radiance. You're resting quietly beside your beloved. Your bodies begin to attune to each other, delicately entwining, ever so lightly at first, then pressing closer together.

Your breath slows down, drifting into an easy rhythmic synchronicity. Notice how your hearts have fallen into rhythm with each other. Can you sense how the very bed you lie on together moves in tandem with the earth's rotation, as if you're both floating in a great ocean together? You feel the urge to share on a deep level arise within you—the urge to share the very core of your being, your essence, your DNA.

"Singing in harmony, can you feel how we are becoming one?"

Seahorses live in an emotionally rich world. Often, they're physically beautiful in a kind of mystical, magical way. When they're happy, they light up and become luminescent. When they're depressed, their inner light dulls and they appear muted and grey, blending into the background. Just as real seahorses change their color to blend with their environment as a survival tactic, *Seahorses* change their facial expressions to match their emotional moods.

As dreamers, *Seahorses* tend to be gentle and kind in spirit. They're often androgynous, especially the males who can be strikingly in touch with their feminine sides. Sometimes this can appear almost too feminine to others. The more masculine female totems can find an interesting balance with androgynous Seahorse male partners.

In the seahorse world, the male seahorse supplies his young with prolactin, the same hormone involved in the production of milk in mammals. For some totem personas, it's just a bit much to see Seahorse men exhibit what's normally considered maternal qualities. However, times have changed, especially with the invention of the baby bottle.

Seahorse males are becoming more in vogue with the advent of the Information Age. Women are finding increasing equality in the work environment with the playing field radically changing and women excelling as breadwinners. In today's world, stay-at-home dads offer workable solutions that never before existed in a significant way.

Seahorses tend to be idealistic in their hopes and desires for a humane world. When these are thwarted, *Seahorses* can resort to escapism. That means they can be secretive at times and often hide their drug, alcohol, and TV addictions. They can become their own worst critics.

Usually versatile and intuitive, *Seahorses* observe and listen well. They can be remarkably creative and excel in literature, music, and art. They're often drawn to partners who are equally passionate about creativity.

"Today is yesterday's tomorrow" is something a *Seahorse* might say. *Seahorses* have the gift of fusing the past with the present and collapsing the perception of time. They are master dreamers, and in dreamtime, anything becomes possible!

An interesting metaphor demonstrating *Seahorses'* ability to attune is seen in sympathetic resonate musical instruments. If you hang two perfectly tuned guitars on opposite walls and then pluck the G string on one of them, the G string on the second guitar hanging on the opposite wall will vibrate synchronistically with the first one.

This same principle allows you to listen to a particular radio station, matching resonate frequencies between your radio and the radio broadcast station. When you adjust the knob on your radio, in effect you change the tension on the receptive frequency receiver to match your favorite radio station's frequency broadcasting band.

Seahorses have this same gift of attuning themselves to others. Keenly aware of frequencies and vibrations, they prefer higher, more refined frequencies. By attuning to others, a deep sense of connection is possible. Feelings of love grow extremely well in this atmosphere.

But herein lies the trap many *Seahorses* find themselves in. Loving to attune to their lovers, they often lose sight of themselves and give up who they are. It's like singing; one person sings a beautiful melody and the second one (the *Seahorse*) sings along in unison, perfectly matching the first voice note for note. In doing so, *Seahorses* lose their sense of a separate self and get lost in another person's song/life. Resentment builds quickly and trouble follows.

The key is to create a harmony that requires *blending* with the first voice but not matching them note for note. Instead, create your own melody—one that harmonizes with the other's song and creates a perfect counterpoint. This allows you to attune to your lover perfectly, perhaps more profoundly. At the same time, it lets you sing your own song, live your own life, and follow your own dreams.

Seahorses in Bed

Real seahorses are magical creatures with an "other worldly" air about them. Delicate in nature, they have an amazing ability to attune to their immediate environment as well as to their partners' surroundings.

Mating pairs of seahorses often morph to bright colors and swim side by side holding tails. They might hold on to the same strand of sea grass with their prehensile tails and spin around in unison in what is known as their pre-dawn dance. This dance can last for hours and sometimes days. In the dance, the male seahorse pumps water through his egg pouch, which expands and opens, displaying his readiness. The female seahorse then carefully deposits her precious eggs into the male seahorse's pouch where they remain until maturity.

It's believed that the seahorse courtship dance evolved over thousands of years to help attune the mating pair for the successful transfer of the precious eggs from the female into the male seahorse's pouch. With the ocean constantly moving and undulating, this transfer could be disastrous if the male and female aren't attuned perfectly. They must move in complete synchronicity with one another.

Seahorses are often androgynous, especially the males. In fact, male seahorses are among the few male animals that actually carry the young through gestation.

Just like their totem, *Seahorses* have an uncanny ability to attune to their lovers. They're delicate in nature and prefer subtle nuances to coarse overtures. In some environments, they can appear to be quite uninterested in sex, but usually it has more to do with their delicate natures than lack of interest. They love to connect, especially on spiritual planes. Consequently, if these refined resonances aren't in place first, *Seahorses* usually become disinterested in sex with that partner.

Often, *Seahorses* have soft, gentle natures and are usually attracted to dynamic partners who can provide the "fire" in the relationship. They're especially drawn to spiritual teachers, political leaders (often human rights advocates), and college professors as well as musicians, painters, and authors. Because highly sensitive *Seahorses* have the ability to attune to their partners, they're often attractive to a variety of the totem personas.

Seahorses tend to give more than they ask for, and in fact, often have difficulty receiving. Highly loyal, they have the ability to endure challenging situations. Compassionate, they want to give the benefit of any doubt to their loved ones.

Reflecting the pre-dawn dance that can last for hours and sometimes days, *Seahorses* have amazing stamina and can often make love for hours and hours despite their naturally delicate nature. Can you hear them whispering? "Let the magic ever be!"

Seahorse's Higher Octave

Seahorses are naturally very sensitive and refined. At core, they embody the ability to attune to their loved ones in a highly empathic manner. At times *Seahorses* may appear to be almost too sensitive and fragile. The invitation for the evolving Seahorse is to place their gaze deep within themselves rather than focusing on pleasing others. Simply by shifting their attention to themselves rather than on how others are feeling, *Seahorses* will find that new possibilities begin to emerge.

You may be pleasantly surprised by how differently others treat you when they sense that you are not always concerned about pleasing them. Letting go of your strong need to feel attuned can initiate a powerful exploration that will help you evolve to a higher octave.

Seahorses are born with sensitive spirits. It's by allowing your natural desire to blend with others to express itself fully, while at the same time deepening your exploration of your own sense of self, that you will truly evolve. Perhaps true harmony is not just simple unison; rather, it is found in the higher octave of counterpoint.

Section II:

Inner

Animal Totems

Inner Animal Totems

The Primary Animal Totems described show how your subject behaves in the physical world. They are determined predominately by the varying physiology of your subject's genitalia. On the other hand, the Inner Animal Totems represent the emotions and the inner qualities of your subject's mind, heart, and spirit.

As noted earlier, the Inner Animal Totems are akin to the Sun Signs in Astrology. Having your subject fill out the Questionnaire Form is the best way to determine which Inner Animal Totem fits best. As a fallback, you can use the subject's birth date.

When giving an in-depth genital reading, it's essential to discover the Inner Animal Totem your subject best matches as well as the Primary Animal Totem. Just as day and night are parts of a full day, Primary and Inner Totems offer different views that help in understanding the whole person.

Again, when the personality type is mentioned, the word is capitalized and in italics; when the real animal is mentioned, it is not.

Rhino (Rinarian)

Rhino: Inner Qualities

Tagline: "Here I come, ready or not!"

Imagine that your energy is so big it could fill a large stadium. Feel the energy of your powerful Rhino horn emanating from the center of your forehead—and sense how strong, how unstoppable you are!

As you flex your sturdy legs, can you feel the overwhelming urge to charge forward? What's that wonderful fragrance coming from the right?

You wheel immediately, changing directions before you charge. It's delicious; you devour it. You raise your head high toward the sky, exhaling with great force, snorting your confidence. You're proud and want all to know that you are standing, breathing, living—right here, right now.

Welcome to the strong, energetic inner world of the Rhino.

Rhinos are exciting, full of life, pulsating with complex emotions. For all their sensitivity about their own feelings, *Rhinos* can be insensitive about other people's feelings.

Rhinos love to charge head on into life and often make immediate decisions. Afterwards, though, they may go through long internal dialogues about their choices. If they don't stay physically active, they can get bogged down with mental regrets.

By nature powerful and strong, *Rhinos* are unstoppable when firing on all cylinders. They often have intelligent, passionate personalities. They're sure of themselves and hard to approach with any different point of view, which makes them great lawyers and debaters.

Rhinos are influenced by Mars and tend to be fearless. They can be quite self-absorbed, often perceiving the world through the filter of their own needs and desires. Prizing directness, they have no patience for dilly-dallying. They're often prideful and would rather be dead than perceived as weak. They tend to find it quite difficult to admit they may have been wrong about anything.

Rhinos love leadership roles and can easily inspire people with their strong convictions and passionate natures. However, they often lack the ability to self-witness and can easily become insensitive to how others are feeling. So caught up in their own inspiration, rarely do they take time to empathize with others. For this reason, they're sometimes difficult to get along with. As a result, they might not be loved and cherished in the way they expect and wish to be.

The tendency to be self-absorbed can work against *Rhinos* especially when they express it as anger and aggression. Often headstrong, they can be quick to get mad. Although capable of holding grudges, more often than not, they're soon off on a new adventure. They don't usually dwell on negative thoughts so long as they can remain physically active. In fact, the key to a *Rhino's* health and happiness is staying extremely physically active.

When the *Rhino* appears as your Inner Quality in a genital reading, know that you likely possess the quality of intensity and the tendency to jump right into the thick of things. On the shadow side, the characteristic of self-absorption can sometimes hinder the depth of connection you so often desire.

Elephant (Elephantarian)

Elephant: Inner Qualities

Tagline: "You are never going to forget me!"

Imagine that your essence is gigantic—enormous. You're totally safe and worry free. If others wanted to harm you, they'd be far too small to do anything that could disturb your sense of peace and tranquility.

Your eyesight is a bit blurry, so you focus on what you're hearing and smelling. Can you feel the vibrations pulsating all around you? Imagine that they're emanating from the earth. Immerse yourself in your sensations. What do you smell right now? What do you hear?

Drop deeper into your awareness and allow yourself to rest in stillness. Let the memories of all the good times you've enjoyed float like clouds through your consciousness. Thoughts of your deep, longtime connections with your family warm your huge heart. Can you smell your family all around you now, hear their breathing, and feel their loving presence?

Reaching up with your trunk, you break off a green branch. Feel how your trunk effortlessly curls toward your mouth, gently grasping the green leafy branch. You chew slowly, savoring the fresh flavors of the abundant earth-food that's always here for you.

Welcome to the tranquil inner world of the Elephant.

Of all the totem types, *Elephants* have the closest relationship with the earth. This inner earth quality forms the core of their being.

On the surface, *Elephants* appear to be forever acquiring possessions and comforts. They're especially attracted to comfort foods and beautiful partners.

When the *Elephant* shows up as the presenting inner quality, know that no matter how many possessions, beautiful partners, or comforts you possess, you may continually find yourself feeling unfulfilled. Through developing your inner connection with the earth and your higher self, a deeper peace can grow. When reading about the qualities of *Elephants*, it's helpful to view everything through this lens.

Elephants hold the medicine of the earth in their huge hearts, which is paramount in their sustenance. Famous for their dependability, *Elephants* offer it freely themselves. When it's not reciprocated, though, watch out! *Elephants* can have terrible tempers.

Elephants don't tend to be talkative, usually demonstrating an economy of language. Rather, they prefer to communicate physically through their actions. They can be highly stubborn once they've grabbed hold of an idea. In their minds, they're being consistent and steady but from the perspective of another, they can appear to be just plain stubborn.

It's never wise to rush an *Elephant* into making a quick decision; it just won't work. *Elephants* need time to think about things, wanting to be absolutely sure before they commit to anything. Once they commit, however, you can depend on them.

Because their essence is so large, *Elephants* tend not to fear big things. If a bear is outside knocking over the garbage can on the back porch, an *Elephant* is sure to march out there, waving and yelling "Shoo!" (Remember, *Elephants* like economy of language.) But say a small yellow jacket bee buzzes around an *Elephant's* face. He or she might freak out, flapping and slapping and running back into the house. *Elephants* despise being accosted by small things.

When the *Elephant* appears as your Inner Quality in a genital reading, know that you possess the quality of being comfortable in your own skin. It feels like the world is at your beck and call, and grace and ease abide within you.

Remember, if you're feeling unfulfilled, seek to create an inner connection with the earth and your higher self.

Chameleon (Chamelaterian)

Chameleon: Inner Qualities

Tagline: "Catch me if you can."

Imagine you're resting on the still, leafy branch of a tree. The warm sun is streaming in through the green leaf light, and you can feel a gentle breeze dancing all about you. You can sense your skin changing color to match the color of the branch on which you lie.

Can you sense how you're becoming invisible to this physical world as you gently close one eye and slip into the dream realm? Dreaming feels so real to you, like pure light. Everything shimmers with a luminescence that sparkles like diamonds. Time has paused for a moment. Can you feel how you're still part of this outer world but at the same time immersed in the dream world? For you, the dream world feels real.

Returning your attention to the physical world, your one closed eye opens again and you realize that your legs are crossed and you've been sitting in a full lotus position meditating. Slowly you open both your eyes even wider and adjust to the light of this world again. The sun shines brilliantly now, warming your inner essence.

Welcome to the inner dream world of the Chameleon.

By their very nature, chameleon lizards are changeable. They tend to morph easily, blending in with their environment. Native Americans believe these lizards live in two worlds. Although they may appear to be asleep, especially when basking in the sun, Native Americans believe they're actually awake, yet dreaming. The chameleon's 360-degree swiveling eyes seem at times to be looking backward inside themselves, as if they're seeing what's to come, dreaming of the future.

A chameleon's skin reflects light and can literally change color so the lizard seems to disappear from this world while still being in it. In Star Trek terms, it's as if chameleons are constantly "phasing" in and out, moving between this world and the others they inhabit.

Like their totem, *Chameleons* live simultaneously in both this world and the dream world. That's why it's so critical for them to be understood in both worlds. Yes, being understood is important to all the 12 totems, but it's especially crucial to *Chameleons* because of their dualistic natures. Simply understanding this duality can sometimes make all the difference.

Most *Chameleons* can process information at double speed. Imagine you're watching a football game and you see a slow motion instant replay of what just happened. Agile *Chameleons* often see the world in sequences like that. Things have to be exceptionally interesting for them to want to stick around. They can get bored easily and often find themselves multi-tasking.

Chameleons often have charming personalities. Extremely facile with language, they love to engage in verbal debate and delight in exchanging ideas.

When the *Chameleon* appears as the main inner quality in a genital reading, know that a high level of versatility is present. Inquisitiveness and a desire to explore are common qualities. So are flexibility and quick-witted intelligence. From the outside, others might experience *Chameleons* as sometimes unreliable, and—if their own desires are involved—they could even accuse their *Chameleon* lover of being capricious.

Chameleons prefer to keep their options open. Like the element mercury, they're bright, shiny, and often quite attractive. However, when you try to connect deeply and grab hold of them, just like mercury, they can slip through your fingers and flow into other worlds.

When the *Chameleon* is viewed as your Inner Totem, know that you're experiencing everything through bifocal lenses, focusing on both this world and the dream world simultaneously.

Possum (Possairian)

Possum: Inner Qualities

**Tagline: "Where is my prince charming/sweet princess?
I will love only the perfect one!"**

Imagine it's nighttime. Gently close your eyes and feel the world around you. Can you sense the influence of the moon? Feel how the different phases of the moon affect your emotions, just as they rule the changing tides. During the brilliance of the full moon, feel how your aliveness expands and, as the moon wanes, how your energy shifts to within.

In the full moon times, feel how you may desire to be highly social, deeply connecting with your wide network of friends and family.

In the inner times of the new moon, feel how your body often wants to disappear, melting into the darkness, allowing you to witness what's happening from a place of safety.

Imagine that the sounds you're now hearing contain a kind of mysterious element. Perhaps it's your prince charming or sweet princess. Can you feel your heart quicken? Now slow down your breathing and become as still as possible. Feel how your body relaxes and presses ever closer to the ground. Can you sense how you're melting into the night? You wait . . . and wait even longer. Is it safe? What's out there?

Strongly influenced by the moon, *Possums* tend to enjoy the nighttime. Complex and imaginative, they're prone to fantasy and may shape their lives to match an ideal they romanticize. *Possums* have better memories than most people and can often remember details about their life as an infant and small child with uncanny accuracy.

Real possums are marsupials and, like all marsupials (such as kangaroos), they carry their young in external pouches during gestation. This fact about their totem animal might partially explain why *Possums* have more vivid early childhood memories than others. It could be that they're actually more present to the outer world during their early development!

When threatened, just like the possum, *Possums* might lash out with clawing and hissing, but they quickly drop into their primary defense strategy, which is withdrawing—and becoming still. *Possums* can become so still, they can appear dead to the world.

At times of stress, *Possums* might be sulky, moody, withdrawn, passive-aggressive, unavailable, and lack normal hygiene. They may not answer their phones or even their own front doors as they feel safer hiding from the world.

Sexually at these times, they can appear lifeless and disinterested. Both male and female *Possums* often act aloof and unapproachable, thus preempting rejection; they are afraid of being vulnerable and exposing their soft, gentle inner nature. When *Possums* feel safe, watch out. Just like the difference between the full and new moon, everything changes; they can become wildly passionate and alive sexually.

Possums often exhibit a tendency to shower love on others in over-compensation. With a tendency to overdo giving, they have difficulty receiving. This is partly because of their generous hearts, but also because they need to overwhelm their lovers and friends with kindness as a smoke screen for hiding their vulnerability and transparency.

Known for being scavengers, real possums are often found at the dump. *Possums* love to scavenge as well, and can spend countless hours at thrift stores sorting through used items to find treasures. When it comes to decorating their homes and adorning their bodies, they prefer antiques to the newest designs. However, when it comes to electronics such as computers and cell phones, they often possess the newest and best model money can buy.

When the *Possum* appears in your genital reading as the Inner Totem, you might see the world as a dangerous and unsafe place. By hiding and retreating into your own inner world, you're resting in a place that feels familiar—a place you know you can trust. Dwelling within, you feel at home and safe. At these times, only the brilliant splendor of the sun, or true love, can reach you.

Remember to breathe deeply. It's essential. Breath, like light, creates the spiritual energy needed to reflect your inner brilliance back into the outer world. Often when you appear to be withdrawn and inaccessible, you're just playing it safe. But inside, you feel wildly alive!

Tiger (Tigarian)

Tiger: Inner Qualities

Tagline: "I'm adorable. Love me!"

Take a deep breath. Imagine you can feel the world through your heart. Sense how your vitality tingles in your warm body and deepens with each breath. How alive you feel! Now allow this feeling to grow and expand into your loins.

Can you feel how your hind legs want to flex? The urge to pounce almost overwhelms you. Something smells incredibly yummy. You can feel your skin quiver. You're excited and totally present. Your eyes are wide open, but more than just seeing, you can smell and hear everything "in living color." No longer able to resist, your legs expand like springs. Feel how your body is now, being propelled forward through the air, tumbling wildly toward ecstasy.

Welcome to the heart-full inner world of the Tiger and family of Big Cats.

Exploring the inner qualities of *Tigers* also touches on the whole family of Big Cats, including lions, cheetahs, cougars, jaguars, and panthers. With core *Tiger* qualities common to all of the Big Cat archetypes, each subspecies adds a slightly different variation to the basic theme. Read through the common inner qualities, then add appropriate specifics for any indicated subspecies.

Tigers strongly reflect characteristics of the sun at the center of this solar system, so it's no surprise they love to be in the middle of everything. They often lead by being right out in front. *Tigers* have huge hearts and are guided by a heart-centered quality more than any other. They're highly intelligent with a strong core and the ability to persevere, even when others have left the fray. Generally easy to read, *Tigers* wear their hearts on their sleeves.

Tigers love nature and feel most at home following their natural instincts. They tend to be loyal, yet because of their passionate nature, they have a strong sexual appetite, which may lead to having affairs. Even so, in their heart of hearts and in their own mind's eye, they remain loyal. At their core, *Tigers* see life as inclusive rather than as an "either/or" proposition. This might not sit well with their partners and friends, who often have definite and differing points of view.

Tigers rely on their open hearts to guide them and thereby might be led to a wide variety of personality types. Unfortunately, being poor judges of character, they sometimes offer their trust to the wrong people. When betrayed or let down, *Tigers* can become disillusioned; they brood. After all, it's hard for them to imagine someone not wanting to align with their vision and direction. Not dealing well with rejection, they take it to heart more than most.

Finding comfort in sharing what they know, *Tigers* love to take on teaching roles. They enjoy expressing their opinions and offer unsolicited advice to anyone willing to listen.

When the *Tiger* shows up in a genital reading as your inner quality, know that heart-fullness, leadership, and generosity prevail.

When the *Cougar* is present, the qualities of "stealth and stalking" become more pronounced. This can be witnessed when "older" *Cougar* women stalk younger men in bar settings. When the *Black Panther* is present, raw power and strength come to the fore. The *Cheetah* embodies the runner who starts out with a burst of energy but lacks stamina and quickly loses interest. With the *Lion*, leadership qualities and family connections are paramount.

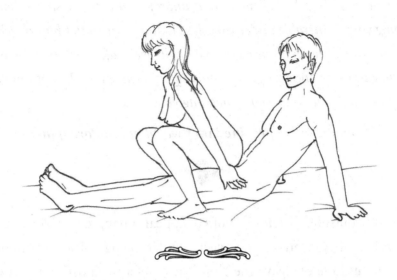

Porcupine (Porcairian)

Porcupine: Inner Qualities

Tagline: "Still waters run deep!"

Imagine that you are sitting in silence. Growing quieter still, you can begin to hear the sound of your own blood pulsating as it flows through your inner ear. Keeping your eyes closed, allow your eyelids to rest gently over your eyes like butterfly wings. Feel how soft your eyes can become.

Next, use your other senses. What do you smell? Can you translate what you smell into a taste? How deep can you explore this inquiry? How many different flavors of smell can you taste?

Listen carefully. How many different sounds can you hear? Are they close or far away? Can you sense their locations? How do they make you feel?

Can you feel your own heart beating? How fast?

Imagine that your skin is covered with sharp thorns facing outward. Only your tender underbelly is smooth and unprotected by these sharp thorns. Keeping your vulnerable underbelly close to the earth, notice how it feels to begin to crawl. Can you sense how your belly feels safe touching the earth?

You hear a new and intriguing sound off in the distance. It captures your attention, and you blink, slowly opening your eyes.

Welcome to the pristine inner world of the Porcupine.

From the outside, *Porcupines* often appear unapproachable, but on the inside, they tend to be sweet, tender beings. They commonly adopt an attitude of "leave me alone" as a defensive posture to protect their sensitive natures. Preferring to keep their feelings close to their chests, they rarely show emotion. *Porcupines* can get preoccupied with cleanliness and keeping things in perfect order. Have you ever watched real porcupines wash (lick) their hands? They're exceedingly patient and do an amazingly thorough job.

Like their animal totem, *Porcupines* tend to move slowly and not rush into new things. Although they demand trust, they rarely offer it easily themselves. They're often wrestling internally with a multitude of self-created conflicts. If you try too quickly to get close to a *Porcupine* who doesn't yet trust you, you're bound to get stuck with a healthy dose of painful "quills."

Porcupines sometimes develop defensive, cold exteriors and at other times they may do 180s and put on overzealous happy faces to accomplish the same task. At all cost, they want to protect their tender, sensitive inner being. Over time, however, this beautiful and often creative inner being can get lost with all these defensive strategies.

One of *Porcupines'* biggest pitfalls is their tendency to keep their guard up all the time. When this happens, they can easily get isolated and become highly critical of both themselves and others. This tendency results from their inclination to worry. *Porcupines* often remain as observers because it feels safe.

When this tendency becomes too pronounced, the shadow side of *Porcupines* becomes apparent. Then the very qualities that work to their benefit—patience, precision, refinement, cleanliness, practicality—turn against them. At these times, *Porcupines* become persnickety, critical, nagging, and neurotic, isolating themselves even more from others.

When the *Porcupine* manifests in a genital reading as your inner quality, know that "still waters run deep" but can also freeze over all too easily. When doing a genital reading for *Porcupines*, it's important to consider age. The older you are, the deeper the sweetness of your true nature may be concealed under the ice. Age can harden your highly effective defenses, both inside and out. Over time, what was once your guardian can turn into your jailer!

The antidote? Remember your youth. By continually working with your inner child and nurturing the soft, sensitive aspects of who you are, your precious inner qualities will, over time, emerge again. Old, deeply buried personal fears could prove to be your biggest demons.

Through patience and the grace of being seen for who you truly are, you can slowly open to love and let your inner light shine through. Know that you can achieve your deepest healing by trusting others and being open to receive love. For you, trust is key!

Dolphin (Dolphinian)

Dolphin: Inner Qualities

Tagline: "Let's play!"

Imagine you're swimming in an expansive, warm ocean. Feel the presence of your loved ones surrounding you. Sense how they make you feel both safe yet free. A cacophony of singing in all directions echoes inside your mind. You smile as you feel overwhelming peace and joy flowing through your being, just knowing you're with your tribe!

Ceasing all movement now, can you feel how your body just wants to float, how you're so beautifully supported by the vast ocean. Can you sense how your body shifts levels as you breathe in and out, gently bobbing up and down with the rhythm of life? Feeling free and supported by all of creation, you begin to sing!

Can you hear how your whole family is singing back to you now? You know that you're not alone!

Welcome to the inner, connected world of the Dolphin.

Dolphins have a deep appreciation for beauty and an overwhelming urge to create beauty in all their relations. Their inner gyroscope helps them stay balanced, no matter how much drama swirls around them.

Just like dolphins, they have the ability to float through life, even when the waters around them are turbulent. As peacemakers of this world, *Dolphins* often sacrifice their own desires to keep things peaceful.

However, if pushed too far—especially if they've tried to keep the peace by sacrificing their own personal needs—*Dolphins* can explode into anger. Normally, they're extremely flexible and allow for great diversity, but like the supple willow tree, they can reach a point of no return and won't allow themselves to be uprooted. When they spring back, their flexibility acts like a bow sending an arrow flying. Their anger magnifies. They can be unexpectedly frightening to others and even to themselves. It's rare, however, for events to escalate to this point, as *Dolphins* are highly amiable by nature and prefer peace and positive vibes.

Dolphins exude sexual energy and love physical contact in a touchy-feely way. They can accept a wider spectrum of lovers than other totem types. They're also less sensitive to smell than many of the other types. (In fact, real dolphins have no sense of smell.)

Highly social, *Dolphins* love to participate in large groups. They're extremely comfortable at events such as concerts, country fairs, and other big gatherings. Because they love to socialize and play, they feel at home in these situations. Conversely, when they're alone, they tend to feel uneasy—like a fish out of water.

Dolphins care about others and naturally want to help people. Mythically, dolphins have been known to help drowning sailors reach the safety of shore. Universally full of heart, they act with compassion when called upon to help humanity. Naturally brave, they willingly face the sharks of life head on, no hesitation.

When the *Dolphin* is your inner quality in a genital reading, know that the spirit of playfulness is being reflected. You carry a light-heartedness as well as a profound desire to help all of humanity.

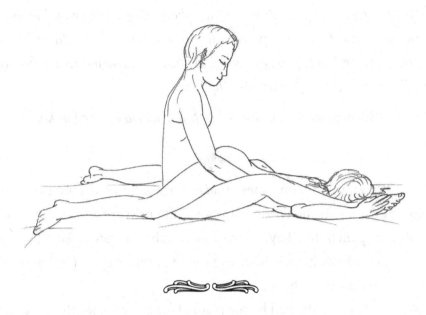

Snake (Snakes)

Snake: Inner Qualities

Tagline: "Come here—I won't bite you."

Imagine you're swimming through waves of deep primal emotions, as if you're on a galactic roller coaster ride. This ride soars to great ecstatic heights, journeying into the heart of ancient mysteries. Then, just as you feel you can't travel any higher, you sense yourself plummeting down into the dark, primordial feelings of sexuality, jealousy, revenge, and the desire for power. Can you feel how your body wants to slowly arch forward naturally supple and flowing with surprising strength and power?

You're keenly aware of your environment and have an uncanny ability to witness your fellow travelers with clarity and a depth that few understand. You long for mastery; you're overwhelmed by the desire to swallow all of existence whole.

You can feel your genitals uncoil now, beginning to tingle and moisten. Can you sense how your power and magnetism pulsate through your entire body and out through your eyes? Your eyes sparkle with fire and intelligence, gazing outward, piercing the world.

Welcome to the mesmerizing inner world of the Snake.

Of all the animal totem types, *Snakes* are the most deeply emotional and exude an unmatched primordial intensity of sexual presence. Their eyes penetrate. They love to look deeply and can make others feel uncomfortable with their intense gaze—a surefire sign of being with a *Snake*! *Snakes* cannot be out-stared.

Snakes are most affected by the planet Pluto, and hence they're drawn to mysteries and love to discover hidden secrets. Highly intelligent and equally patient, they can wait long periods to act—just like a rattlesnake might wait under the same rock for hours, even days, for an auspicious moment to strike.

Snakes value loyalty above all else. They may perceive betrayal in the slightest nonalignment of another with their understanding of the way things should be. And when they feel betrayed, their emotional reaction is often intense.

Independent and self-contained, *Snakes* almost always know who they are; opinions others have of them (good or bad) mean very little. Personal power lies at the heart of their motivation. Consummate dealmakers, they have a high regard for themselves and always watch for an edge that can give them more power.

When positive, *Snakes* use their personal power for the betterment of humankind; when negative, they can express their personal power in deeply dark ways.

Quite secretive, *Snakes* often have a cool outer quality, rarely showing what they feel inside. But don't be deceived by their calm, even demeanors. Underneath, intense feelings are often brewing. It's not their nature to reveal their own feelings but to penetrate the depths of those around them so they know how others feel. This is a primary strategy for gaining power over others. With their penetrating eyes, they rarely miss a thing.

With their sexuality full of deep feeling, they love to jump in wholeheartedly. Just as snakes swallow their prey whole, *Snakes* jump into their sexual attractions fully—with body, mind, and soul.

Although they're highly physical, *Snakes* are drawn to the mystical and spiritual qualities of love. They often experience their deepest connection in stillness because it opens doorways to a rich array of emotional and mystical experiences.

Snakes demand total loyalty and devotion from their lovers and partners but rarely offer the same in return. For the most part, they're loyal—after a fashion. They love to flirt and exercise their powers of magnetism, leading to nothing more—most times. *Snakes* love secrets and can rationalize deeper connections with others as being special or different. Yet they won't tolerate the same behavior in their partners.

Snakes are drawn to participate in battles, especially those requiring subtle strategy and keen intelligence. They tend to be fearless, willing to jump into the fray and engage.

Naturally possessing a deep knowing of the mysteries of life, *Snakes* often have a mystical understanding of the circle of life and death. The symbol of the snake eating its own tail is highly significant. *Snakes* realize they can "shed their skins" and be reborn, yet some part of their essence remains constant through each shedding.

Interestingly, snakes in the animal kingdom don't shed the skin covering their eyes. Their eyes cloud over during the shedding process and they're blind for a brief moment, but their eyes remain the same and no new skin is formed over them. Look at a snakeskin that's been shed and you'll find holes where the snake's eyes were. In this sense, with each new shedding of the old skin, the snake's eyes remain constant. *Snakes* see the world through these constant, unchanging, ancient eyes, which explains why their eyes can be so piercing.

When the *Snake* comes up as your inner totem in a genital reading, pay special attention to how you use your energy. *Snakes* are extremely powerful, and their energy can easily slip into the shadow side of life. The key is to always stay in touch with your remarkable flexibility. This quality allows you to remember you have various options always available to you. Choose to use your abundant power for good. Know that your sexual energy strongly affects others.

When the *Boa* is evident in a genital reading as part of your Inner *Snake* archetype, you might be more inclined to encircle others. *Boas* know that, by forming concentric coils of their energy around any situation—physical, spiritual, or emotional—they can control the situation and outcome over time.

When the *Rattlesnake* is evident, you could be inclined to coil, creating tension like a spring, ready to strike out with intensity. On a spiritual plane, you have the ability to pierce the illusion of life and death, always finding the truth at the heart of any situation.

When the *King Snake* is evident, you might be inclined to feign the appearance of danger, just as the king snake mimics the pattern of circular bands seen on the dangerous coral snake's skin. *King Snakes* often use their power for protection and extend it by transforming themselves into warrior heroes, defending the weak and defenseless, especially the young. A *King Snake* almost always prevails over an adversary, no matter how dangerous.

Frog/Toad (Frogarian)

Frog/Toad: Inner Qualities

Tagline: "Kiss me; I'm really a prince/princess!"

Imagine you're squatting close to the ground. Your skin feels dry so you glide into the cool water lapping at your toes. You stretch out, reaching forward with your arms while allowing your legs to gently push back. You hover there for a moment, floating, drifting, being supported by the buoyant water. You feel totally comfortable inside your own skin. You've journeyed deep into your soul, into the mysteries of life and death, and felt your own transformation from within.

Your eyes are half underwater and half above the surface. You can see a split-image view of the land and under the water at the same time—like a Wyland painting. This expanded view of seeing both worlds simultaneously truly amazes you.

You are happy to rest inside your own being. Yet, at the same time, something inside you wants to share this beautiful vision with another, so your eyes comb the horizon to see who may be present. Far off in the distance, you hear the melodious song of your potential lover floating out into the twilight. The song echoes inside your soul, and you feel your strong legs thrusting behind you now as you glide through the water, singing in harmony with your newfound love.

Welcome to the inner mystical world of the Frog.

Optimistic and good natured, *Frogs* like to see the positive sides of things. Inter-dimensional in their awareness, they carry the quality of inner magic. Metamorphosis is the key focus of a *Frog's* journey.

It has been said of people in general that "some grow—and some just grow old!" This especially applies to people of the *Frog* totem. Some *Frogs* never pass through the pollywog stage, so living in water is the only world they know. As a result, they remain linear in their perceptions, preferring to live on the surface of life.

The evolved *Frog* archetype often goes through a true metamorphosis, like surviving a life-threatening disease or car accident, the loss of a partner, or other kinds of life-changing experiences. As a result, they grow into transformed beings with expansive qualities. Their metamorphosis allows them to span different realities—which makes them highly attractive to others. Evolved *Frogs* often find other beings drawn to their deeper knowing of the mystical realms and their comfort level with issues of life and death.

Because of their deep inner knowing and wealth of personal experience, *Frogs* can be quite philosophical. They tend to be extremely sensitive to their environment in the present moment. They can sense how others are feeling, both on a one-to-one basis and in group settings. For all their sensitivity, *Frogs*—like their totem animal—have one key blind spot, which is their perception of time.

Real frogs are known to quickly jump out of a pot of boiling hot water when placed in it to be cooked. But if a frog is put into warm water first and the water heated gradually, the frog may not notice the increasing heat. It's likely to remain in the pot until it dies from the heat. Even though this folklore belief may not be scientifically true, it seems to be metaphorically true for *Frog* archetypes. This can be seen happening to *Frogs* in long-term relationships that change ever so slowly. *Frogs* tend to stick around long after the love has evaporated and the relationship has deteriorated into an unhealthy attachment.

When the *Frog* is found to be your inner quality in a genital reading, know that the idea of metamorphosis is important for you to explore. Pay attention to your magical qualities in the intimate realm and the depth of your true knowing, which comes from your soul's inner journey.

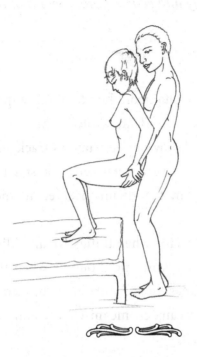

Turtle/Tortoise (Terrapin)

Turtle/Tortoise: Inner Qualities

Tagline: "Step by step . . . I am victorious!"

Imagine that time has slowed down and you're living your life as if in slow motion. You're well acquainted with your surroundings; you have anticipated and prepared well for this journey—no surprises. You plan to live here for a very, very long time.

You can feel you're being protected by an impenetrable shell, and this sense of being safe allows you to relax. Quietly, you focus on what you really want. You feel confident and know you can manifest anything your heart desires. Keeping your eye on your goal, you move steadily in that direction.

Welcome to the steady and reliable inner world of the Turtle.

Turtles are extremely self-contained. They tend to be quite steady and practical. Usually, they're confident, skilled, shrewd, strong-willed, and calm by nature. They know how to stay on track and are good at completing projects. They have a keen sense of smell and excellent eyesight, which allows them to remain oriented in most situations. *Turtles* stay on course.

Although confident, especially when things are unfolding as planned, *Turtles* can easily slip into pessimistic thoughts when things don't go as they expect. At these times, their Saturnine nature compels them to recede into their shell. They can become miserly, resentful, fatalistic, and possibly even mean-spirited.

Have you ever placed your finger in front of a snapping turtle? Well, it's not a good idea!

Usually, though, *Turtles* are good natured. They often have a wry, dry sense of humor that they alone appreciate.

Turtles love to acquire knowledge and often excel in school, frequently returning in their later years to develop new skill sets. They use their knowledge in two ways: (1) to navigate the pathways of life in a skillful and patient manner and (2) to protect themselves from bad experiences. Sometimes they use their continual studying as a shield against strong emotions so they feel less vulnerable. They're often quite concerned about financial security.

Turtles tend to live a long time. They remain calm in the knowledge that, at any time, they can safely retreat into their impenetrable shells and patiently wait things out.

Have you ever seen sea turtles eat seaweed? They chew each bite incredibly slowly. Now, there's a valuable hint in how to extend your life! *Turtles* seem to move to a different tempo than others. They not only eat each bite of food slowly and deliberately but consume all forms of nourishment that way, including love. They savor each lovemaking moment fully!

As parents, *Turtles* may appear less emotionally involved than many of the other totem types. Real turtles lay their eggs in the sand and often never see their young again, forcing them to fend for themselves. Of course, this would be an extreme exaggeration for *Turtles*, but one aspect of this can be seen in their unwillingness to get too emotionally involved with their children. This often reflects their need to stay calm and not be vulnerable. Sometimes *Turtles* act in the exact opposite manner and become so involved with their children, they allow them to become their whole focus. This is especially common if the *Turtle* is a single parent or only has one child.

In numerous cultures, turtles are portrayed carrying the world on their backs. The Earth is known to the indigenous people in North America as Turtle Island. The turtle carries its home on its back wherever it goes. Likewise, *Turtles* feel at home wherever they are. They move slowly and calmly through life with a deep sense of knowing who they are.

When the *Turtle* is identified as your inner quality in a genital reading, know that you value the qualities of steadiness and consistency. You tend to skillfully avoid emotional dramas. Most important, you often end up succeeding in what you begin.

Pheasant/Peacock (Peacoshian)

Pheasant/Peacock: Inner Qualities

Tagline: "I'm beautiful. Look at me!"

Imagine you're living in a place where everyone is truthful. You feel at home just knowing everyone is connected in a higher truth. Your eyes perceive your own beauty and the beauty that surrounds you. You have a deep love for all humanity and can feel the interconnectedness of life. As the sun rises, you bask in its golden illumination, knowing a new age is at hand. You spread out your brilliant-colored tail feathers, each one possessing a magical eye, reflecting your ability to see all aspects of every situation. You breathe deeply, happy in your knowing of self and of your ability to be alone as well as with others.

Welcome to the inner humanitarian world of the Peacock.

Peacocks revere truth above all else. They're leaders and often visionaries who love to call others together, especially for humanitarian endeavors. *Peacocks* enjoy their hours alone and often need time for introspection. Fiercely independent, they participate best in groups if they lead the way; they're not good followers.

Peacocks love to keep things vague, especially when asked to set precise times for appointments. Forget about setting appointments by the hour; even finding a particular day can be difficult. Sometimes "this week" is the closest commitment a *Peacock* is likely to make.

As champions of the people, *Peacocks* stand on a soapbox and passionately expound on their vision of truth and justice. They're often stunningly beautiful or handsome. To witness a *Peacock* is to perceive heaven on earth.

When the *Peacock* is seen as the inner quality in your genital reading, at play is the quality of the All Seeing Eye, which sees multiple perspectives simultaneously. In love, you are often drawn to agape love rather than romantic love.

You have a true visionary quality and good intentions for all humanity. When things do not unfold in the way you may have envisioned, be on guard for a sharp tone of voice that might suddenly come from your own lips.

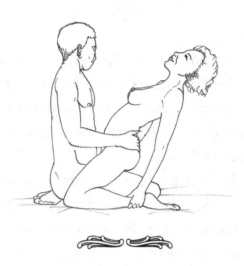

Seahorse (Sea-airian)

Seahorse: Inner Qualities

Tagline: "Let the magic ever be."

Imagine you're floating in a warm sea of embryonic fluid. Luminescent light filters into your eyes with a soft radiance from above. You feel (more than you can see) your beloved beside you. Your hands clasp; your arms gently twist together in a delicate prehensile tail-like embrace. Your bodies slowly sway in rhythm with each other. Your motion expands now, and soon you acrobatically spin and swirl in perfect unison. You can deeply feel your connection with each other; your hearts beat as one in this pre-dawn dance. You can feel your profound alignment with all of life.

Welcome to the inner intuitive world of the Seahorse.

The *Seahorses'* greatest gift is their ability to attune to many diverse environments. Just like *Chameleons*, they have the ability to change color and blend perfectly with their surroundings. Yet *Seahorses* take merging one step further. They have the ability to move gracefully and come together with their partners, complementing them in creating a blended life together. Their gentle spirits, absence of hidden agendas, and ability to adjust allow them to merge with a wide variety of totem types. Because they often lack fire, they are drawn to fiery partners who balance them in this way. They rarely take on leadership roles, preferring to support and nurture. Drawn to making their living as artists, they can be autonomous this way, which suits them well.

Seahorses care deeply for others and often get involved in the helping professions. Sometimes they help family members and loved ones so much, they disregard their own needs. Deeply compassionate, *Seahorses* support just causes and care for children and the elderly.

Seahorses often seem to be in another world. They tend to move slowly, almost cat-like, and while they're physically in this world, they sense the presence of something else that's simultaneously taking place on another plane.

Sometimes the stress and craziness of the world can be too much for them. At these times, *Seahorses* can fall into their shadow side and seek escapes. They have a tendency to use recreational drugs, alcohol, and TV to escape what are usually self-created pressures. When indulging in their preferred avenue of escape, they often choose to be secretive, not wanting others to know what they are up to.

Even though *Seahorses* are often their own biggest critic, they don't want to hear criticism from anyone else, especially from friends and family members. Highly idealistic, they become secretive about doing the things they themselves often judge.

They tend to see the positive side of life, preferring to wear rose-colored glasses at times. A strong Neptune influence can be seen in their watery, dreamy eyes. These eyes often have an uncanny ability to see into the future, so if a *Seahorse* has a premonition, consider it a possibility.

Seahorses frequently show sweet demeanors. They're often attractive to others and have a soft, gentle quality about them. This especially stands out in male *Seahorses*, who often have highly developed feminine sides.

They can be highly emotional and their tears flow easily. Because they feel life deeply, they can swing between highs and lows in short periods.

When the *Seahorse* is seen as the inner quality in your genital reading, know that your ability to attune to other people is highly refined. You are drawn to creative people and repelled by coarse or crude actions and language. Pay special attention to your desire to escape the stresses and pressures of this world. Seek healthy choices that can relieve the stress of life while simultaneously satisfying your attraction for escape.

The following poem beautifully captures the spirit of Seahorses:

Avani

It was Friday night like so many others
People were sliding across the dance floor
Rhythmically moving through space and time
When, unnoticed, an attractive man arrived

His body married to a chair on wheels
Yet his eyes spoke of light and spirit
Things beyond this world
He entered, arms swaying to the pulse of the music
Expertly spinning on one wheel
Then reversing again, flowing with the dancers

Part of the dance, yet not
Like some kind of broken winged bird
A smile painted on his face
Saying, "I too can be part of this"
Yet his eyes spoke of a loneliness
We can each know, only in our own way

Silently in the corner of the room, she began to move
Slowly and passionately with a grace true dancers know
Each movement full of feeling
In every slow articulation of every shifting muscle
Her being present with total commitment

With the heart of true compassion
She begins to dance with the wheelchair man
Not like the others, waving their arms superficially
Smiling and quickly moving on
But deeply from the soul
Like a lover total and whole

It took a while for him to catch on
And stop waving his hands
Stop smiling like cardboard
To begin to relax
And receive this alive gift of being

They looked as if they were in slow motion
Moving in a different time and space than the others
Like a still point inside a blur of motion
Moving slowly in unison as one

The chair no more separate
Only a man and a woman
Moving deeply from within
The smile melting into the real

The woman held in his arms now, as if a lover
Slowly sliding around his body like a silk scarf

With utmost care, as a diver on the high board
She holds herself in suspension, a handstand, upside down
Hands on the wheelchair
Body arching

Ever so gently, eyes wide open
Lowering herself, like a swan in slow motion
Her hair softly cascading in his lap
Arching forward and back up again
For a moment, there is no chair
There is no time
No room
Only the quiet explosion of a compassionate heart
Of the dancers becoming the dance

And for a moment
We, with our invisible wheelchairs
Feel renewed
Touched and passionately alive

   – Aiden Talinggers

Section III:

Further Influences -

Animal Totems

Further Influences – Animal Totems

Through basic visual observation, you can easily determine Further Influences. They apply predominately to the Primary Animal Totems section in a genital reading.

When experienced readers give personal readings, Further Influences can also be applied to the Inner Animal Totems section, but having a second-party perspective is essential to succeed at this. In performing self-readings, the Further Influences section *exclusively* applies to the Primary Animal Totems section—that is, unless you have access to a computer with the Genital Reading's proprietary Questionnaire software for determining the Further Influences Inner Animal Totems.

When determining the subject's Primary Animal Totem, often one animal totem is not 100 percent clear. Usually one choice stands out, but aspects of some of the other animal totems may also be present. This is when the Further Influences section comes into play.

Once you pick one of the 12 animal totems that best represents your subject's Primary Animal Totem, other animal totems can be considered, too. These fall under the jurisdiction of the Further Influences section. It is best to limit these to one Further Influence, at the most two. Through practice and careful observation, the Further Influences will become easy to identify.

Rhino (Rinarian)

Further Influences: When the *Rhino* is a secondary component of a reading, it often reflects the characteristic of charging headfirst into any circumstance. Are there certain situations in your life where a more assertive behavior sometimes emerges?

Make a point of asking these questions to reveal insights:

- Where or when in my life do I tend to be outrageous? How does this serve or disserve me?

- Do I find myself becoming more adventurous and fearless than usual in certain situations? How do these qualities expand my life?

Elephant (Elephantarian)

Further Influences: When the *Elephant* is a secondary component of a genital reading, often the quality of steadfastness is a key characteristic. Are there certain situations in your life where you find yourself becoming reliable?

Make a point of asking these questions to reveal insights:

- Where or when in my life do I tend to be dependable? How does this serve or disserve me?

- Do I find myself becoming more steady and consistent than usual in certain situations? How can these qualities temper my life?

Chameleon (Chamelaterian)

Further Influences: When the *Chameleon* is a secondary component of a genital reading, often a key consideration is the quality of changeability. Are there certain situations in your life where you experience more versatility?

Make a point of asking these questions to reveal additional insights:

- Where or when in my life do I tend to vacillate and be changeable? How does this serve or disserve me?

- Do I find myself becoming more curious and inquisitive than usual in certain situations? How do these qualities expand or affect my life?

Possum (Possairian)

Further Influences: When the *Possum* is a secondary component of a genital reading, key qualities are emotionally and/or physically playing dead. Are there certain situations in your life where you want to hide and feel invisible?

Make a point of asking these questions to reveal additional insights:

- Where or when in my life do I tend to retreat and hide? How does this serve or disserve me?

- Do I find myself becoming more fearful and cautious than usual in certain situations? How do these qualities affect my life?

Tiger (Tigarian)

Further Influences: When the *Tiger* is a secondary component of a genital reading, key are the qualities of magnetism and heart-fullness. Are there certain situations in your life where you tend to feel friendly and welcoming?

Make a point of asking these questions to reveal additional insights:

- Where or when in my life do I tend to open up and trust others? How does this serve or disserve me?

- Do I find myself becoming more trusting and welcoming than usual in certain situations? How do these qualities affect my life?

Porcupine (Porcairian)

Further Influences: When the *Porcupine* is a secondary component of a genital reading, key is the quality of protectiveness. Are there certain situations in your life where you tend to become unapproachable and guarded?

Make a point of asking these questions to reveal additional insights:

- Where or when in my life do I tend to contract and be more guarded? How does this serve or disserve me?

- Do I find myself becoming more of a perfectionist in certain situations? How does this quality affect my life?

Dolphin (Dolphinian)

Further Influences: When the *Dolphin* is a secondary component of a genital reading, key is the quality of playfulness. Are there certain situations in your life where you tend to feel more playful?

Make a point of asking these questions to reveal additional insights:

- Where or when in my life do I tend to be playful? How does this serve or disserve me?

- Do I find myself becoming more playful and joyful than usual in certain situations? How can these qualities affect my life?

Snake (Snakes)

Further Influences: When the *Snake* is a secondary component of a genital reading, key are the qualities of intelligence, magnetism, sexuality, and secretiveness. Are there certain circumstances in your life where you feel secretive or mysterious?

Make a point of asking these questions to reveal additional insights:

- Where or when in my life do I tend to be secretive? How does this serve or disserve me?

- Do I find myself becoming more mysterious than usual in certain situations? How does this affect the quality of my life?

- Do I find myself becoming more sexual than usual in certain situations? How does this affect the quality of my life?

Frog/Toad (Frogarian)

Further Influences: When the *Frog/Toad* is a secondary component of a genital reading, key is the quality of metamorphosis. Are there certain situations in your life where you may be more open to change?

Make a point of asking these questions to reveal additional insights:

- Where or when in my life might I be open to a metamorphosis? How can this serve or disserve me?

- Do I find myself becoming more open to changes than usual in certain situations? In what way does this quality enhance my life?

Turtle/Tortoise (Terrapin)

Further Influences: When the *Turtle* is a secondary component of a genital reading, key are the qualities of patience and self-containment. Are there certain situations in your life where you tend to be more private and self-contained?

Make a point of asking these questions to reveal additional insights:

- Where or when in my life do I find myself needing more privacy? How could this serve or disserve me?

- Do I find myself becoming more self-contained and patient than usual in certain situations? How do these qualities enhance my life?

Pheasant/Peacock (Peacoshian)

Further Influences: When the *Pheasant/Peacock* is a secondary component of a genital reading, key is the quality of agape (that is, love for all humanity rather than a particular person). Are there certain situations in your life where you find yourself becoming more interested in love for all humanity?

Make a point of asking these questions to reveal additional insights:

- Where or when in my life do I find myself being more open-minded about universal love? How can this serve or disserve me?

- Do I find myself becoming more accepting of all of humanity in certain situations? How can this quality enhance my life?

- If I'm often driven by the ups and downs of romantic love, are there times in my life when agape love feels equally important? How does this feel?

Seahorse (Sea-airian)

Further Influences: When the *Seahorse* is a secondary component of a genital reading, key are the qualities of sensitivity and intuition. Are there certain situations in your life where you find yourself becoming more sensitive to what is happening around you?

Make a point of asking these questions to reveal additional insights:

- Where or when in my life do I tend to be more selfless? How can this serve or disserve me?

- Do I find myself becoming more sensitive and intuitive than usual in certain situations? How do these qualities expand my life?

Section IV:

Love Positions

Animal Totems

Love Positions – Animal Totems

Okay, it's time to have fun! The Love Positions are just the kind of "homework" you always dreamed about having in college!

Each of the 12 Animal Totems has four preferred love positions, which correspond to the Primary Animal Totem. Simply put, if your Primary Animal Totem is a *Seahorse*, your four Love Positions to practice initially are those of the *Seahorse*.

After exploring your totem's favorite Love Positions, experiment with different totems' Love Positions. Better yet, try them all! Each day, read the attributes pertaining to the Animal Totem Love Position you wish to engage in. The more Animal Totems and their preferred Love Positions you explore, the richer your lovemaking experience will become. (Note: See www.SignsOfIntimacy.com) for news of the release of the second book in this series with a companion card deck dedicated to deepening this exploration.)

Rhino Love Positions (Rinarian)

R hinos infuse their love positions with confidence.

They jump into lovemaking with natural enthusiasm, often initiating love encounters. With their strong physicality and high-voltage energy, they're straightforward in letting their lovers know exactly how they feel.

Rhinos aren't interested in subtle nuances, exotic positions, or mastering skills. Rather than study and practice Tantra like *Turtles*, they love getting right into action. Because of their physicality and the force of their passion, they naturally find themselves in unique, interesting embraces.

When exploring the *Rhino's* essence and how it can expand your lovemaking, practice the four preferred Rhino positions shown and pay special attention to these suggestions:

1. Let your natural sexual energy effortlessly arise within. Explore the feeling of being truly desired, even if this is not your natural belief. Allow yourself to let go of all your preconceived ideas and jump

headfirst into your attractions, no hesitation. Let your passion arise from within and lead you forward. (Remember, *Rhinos* charge headfirst into life.)

2. Sense how your natural physical prowess is contagious, how it affects your lover. Marvel at the new love positions your inner passion guides you into unexpectedly.

Rhinos are blessed with the ability to help their lovers jump into lovemaking without inhibition through their infectious exuberance. Allow the power of feeling totally confident to infuse and expand your understanding of yourself.

Rhino Love Positions

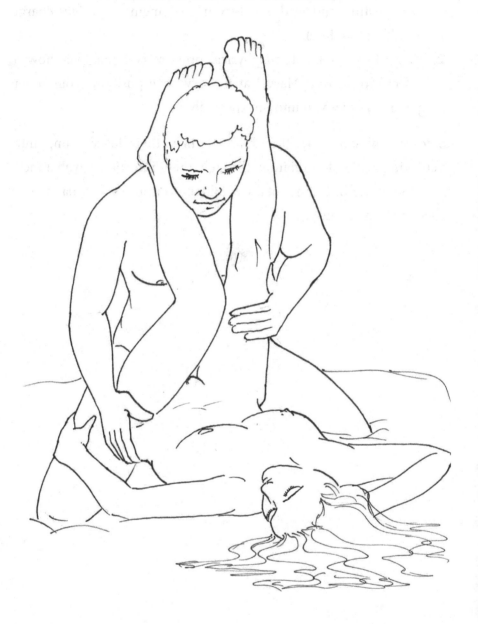

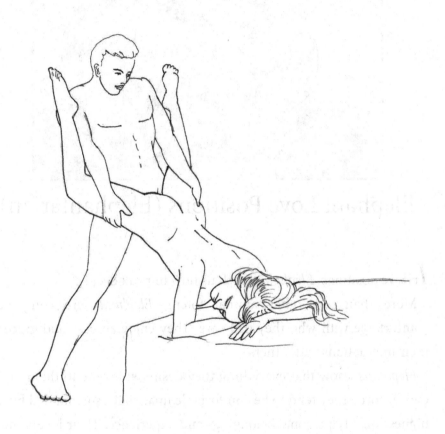

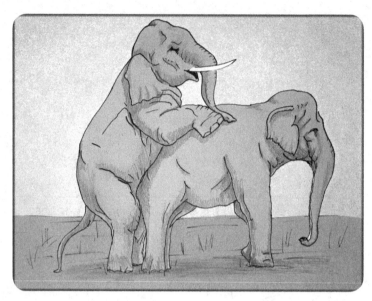

Elephant Love Positions (Elephantarian)

*I*n love positions, *Elephants* teach us how to relax deeply.

More than any other animal totem, *Elephants* are completely comfortable with who they truly are. They enjoy an ease and grace in their interactions with others.

Elephants know that everything they desire will come to them on its own accord. They tend to be comfortable financially, surrounded by the highest quality personal belongings and experience. Their lovers move toward them with little effort on their part.

Because others are naturally attracted to them, *Elephants* don't have to go through a lot of motions to realize their desires. Often uninterested in manipulating their courtships, they prefer to allow events to unfold organically with minimal effort. Similarly, they tend to keep their love positions simple and direct.

When exploring the *Elephant's* essence and how it can expand your lovemaking, practice the four preferred *Elephant* positions shown and pay special attention to these suggestions:

1. Sense that you are perfect exactly how you are, that you don't have to do anything to find love. Allow this feeling of ease to permeate your entire body. Slowly and easily, start to move toward your lover. Feel how your presence alone draws that person closer to you in a warm, effortless way.

2. Elephants have amazing noses (trunks) that serve many functions. Gently rub your lover's nose with your nose, just like Eskimos do in greeting. *Elephants* can feel extremely close just sharing this simple gesture. When *Elephants* are connecting, emotional bonding sometimes far exceeds physical climax.

3. *Elephants* themselves are profoundly connected to the earth. When exploring *Elephant* love positions, place your attention on how you also connect with the earth. Discern which part of your body is touching the ground/bed. Feel how you can literally draw energy up through these points of contact from the infinite energy source of the earth, thus energizing you in unlimited ways.

Elephant energy will ground you to the earth and show you how comfortable life can be. So relax, tap into the infinite energy always abounding from the earth, and enjoy the ride!

Elephant Love Positions

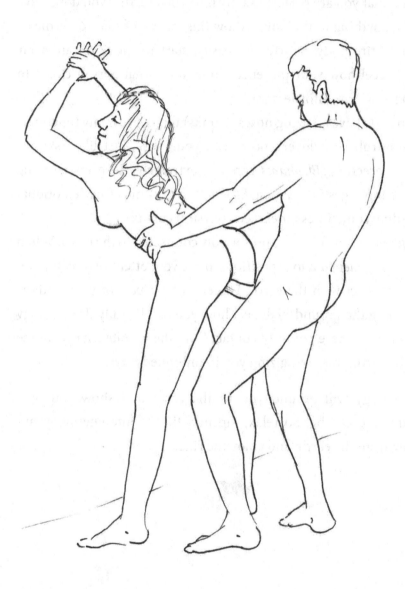

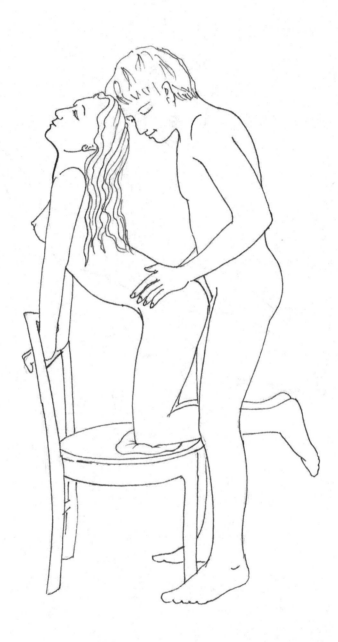

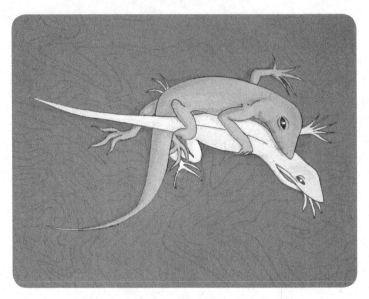

Chameleon Love Positions
(Chamelaterian)

Chameleons imbue their love positions with the quality of receiving energy and reflecting it back amplified. They embody the intrinsic properties of mercury in their mirroring and quick movements. With one foot in the dream world, *Chameleons* can easily slide into the realm of fantasy.

Although love positions focus on physical postures, it's just as important to investigate what's going on in your partner's head. *Chameleons* tend to place more attention on the mental than the physical. Thus, they enjoy the art of fantasy play and mastering disguise. This can become just as exciting as the physical act of making love.

Real chameleons morph to blend with their environment, their very skin changing colors. Similarly, life is a theater for *Chameleons*, masters of change and acting. They love to play different roles and can slip into entirely new dramas with grace and ease. Their mercurial natures are perfectly suited for constant change, which they dearly love.

Real chameleons have amazing tongues—essential to their ability to survive. *Chameleons* have wonderful tongues as well. They revel in verbal banter and they equally love kissing. In fact, they can be happy kissing for hours and feel complete with just that!

Chameleon love positions are basic because *Chameleons* prefer full-body contact with their partners; physical contact helps them feel what their lovers are feeling. They love to take this energy in, amplify it inside themselves, and then reflect it back.

When exploring the *Chameleon's* essence and how it can expand your lovemaking, practice the four different *Chameleon* positions shown. But rather than focus on the physical positions, shift your awareness to your mind.

While practicing these positions, align your awareness with these inquiries:

1. How am I feeling? Can I sense my lover approaching? What mood is he/she in? How can I blend with his/her energy? Can I amplify this energy? How far can we let our energies rise together? Is my skin starting to tingle, reflecting our love?

2. How close can I press my body to my lover's? We're just breathing now. Lying still, can we enter into dream space together? Are pictures of the future arising? How present am I? Is my mind already slipping away?

3. Who can we be tonight? How fun it feels to dress up. I love playing fantasy.

Chameleons have the ability to help you *not* take yourself too seriously. As they live in the present, they gather their energy from it. They reflect life like diamond facets in their ever-changing luminous skin. For this moment, you may mean the world to them. But as quickly as the wind changes direction, they may be off reflecting the beauty of someone else just as sincerely. Can you be okay with this?

How does it feel exploring this animal totem quality inside yourself? Who would you be if you lived your life without your story, if you lived spontaneously? What else is possible?

Chameleon Love Positions

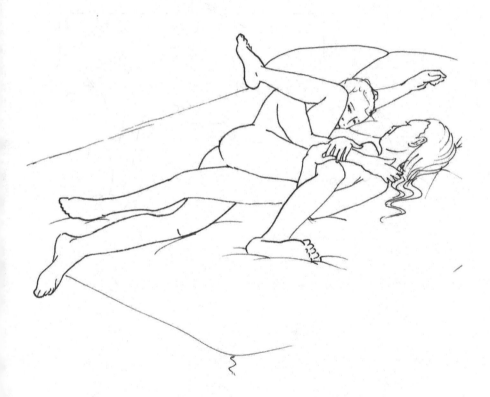

Possum Love Positions (Possairian)

*T*he *Possum's* essence in love positions is about viewing sexuality from fresh new perspectives.

Seeing the world from their unique vantage point, *Possums* place their attention on their spiritual and emotional being rather than physical qualities. Often, they care more about relationships than things. Possessing incredible memories, they cherish their past deep emotional and spiritual connections.

At first, *Possums* might not appear interested in connecting sexually. Male *Possums* can have difficulty sustaining erections or ejaculate too quickly; female *Possums* may not be orgasmic or may be completely shut down to touch. This reflects their affiliation with their animal totem, the possum, which plays dead but is actually fully alive. Sometimes, this behavior is linked to an old wound or a core fear.

Because *Possums* carry this energy, they've learned to redirect their sexual energies into creative expressions as well as deeply spiritual pursuits. In their efforts to balance their lives, they've learned to see the world differently than others.

Connected to the phases of the moon, *Possums* are highly emotional and show a wide range of expression. Sexually, *Possums* tend to love oral sex because it feels safe and fewer performance issues arise. They feel truly cared for, secure, and wanted, allowing them to open up, thus quelling their fears and deepening their relationships.

Possums can connect just as deeply by meditating with their beloved. Frequently, they prefer meditating together rather than having sex.

When exploring the *Possum's* essence and how it can expand your lovemaking, practice the four different preferred *Possum* positions shown and pay special attention to these suggestions:

1. Focus on feeling emotionally connected with your lover. Allow your desire to feel safe to be okay. How deeply can you relax into receiving? Slip into "being" rather than "doing," and let go of any need to perform. View the sex act as "giving" rather than "taking." Feel your own love well up inside so strongly that your only thought is to adore your beloved in all ways possible. Open your mouth and receive, just like when you were first born. Join with the source of all life.

2. Let all your thoughts dissolve into the mystery of life. How still can you be? Let go of the past, let go of the future, be here now. While practicing the *Possum* love positions, know that no matter what's

happening externally, some part of you is always aware, witnessing everything. Know that this witness is your true being.

Possums can help you release your preconceived ideas about how to make love. Simply empty your mind and just "be" with whatever is in the moment.

Possum Love Positions

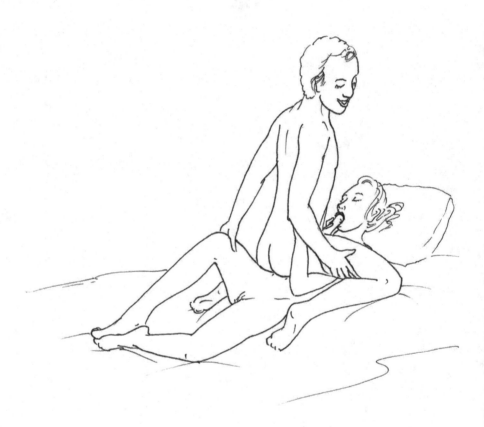

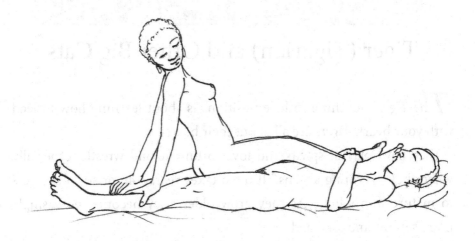

Tiger (Tigarian) and Other Big Cats

*T*he *Tigers'* teaching in love positions is about learning how to lead with your heart. *Tigers* are all about their hearts.

They have playful spirits and love to tumble and wrestle, especially when they're "young kittens." It often takes years—40 or so—for *Tigers* to mature into adults. As they grow older, they become increasingly more serious and attached.

Tigers love to have their hearts facing their lover. Being highly visual, they have extremely keen eyesight. Because they're attracted to physical beauty, they prefer to see their lover's face. Hence, they tend to enjoy love positions in which they can see their lovers' faces as well as feel their hearts. For *Tigers*, physical attraction is important, but surprisingly, they aren't particularly comfortable with eye contact.

Tigers love foreplay. They're enormously physical and love to play, wrestle, roll around, and lick their lovers all over. *Tigers* feel the world with their tongues.

They also are flexible in their bodies and often find themselves in fun, interesting, and exotic love positions. Sometimes they can get so lost in their play, they forget about their preferred heart-to-heart, face-to-face love positions and end up in quite surprising positions. This is frequently due to the innate need for all *Tigers* to let go of their minds and experience the sublime. Play and laughter help *Tigers* jump through this portal.

When exploring the *Tiger's* essence and how it can expand your lovemaking, practice the four preferred *Tiger* positions shown and pay special attention to these suggestions:

1. Feel how your intrinsic animal magnetism draws your lover close to you. Look upon the face of your beloved and feel your heartbeat quicken. Feel how oxygen-rich red blood pulsates toward your loins as if your genitals were a natural extension of your heart, pulsating and expanding. Can you feel how your body has that overwhelming urge to pounce? Before you realize it, you're flying through the air, tumbling forward into ecstasy.

2. Notice how your own body feels supple yet strong. Can you sense your kitten spirit arise—just wanting to play? How fun it feels to tumble and roll around with your beloved. Marvel in the interesting new love positions your inner play spirit has led you into unexpectedly!

Tigers can help you learn to lead with your heart, to play, to have fun just for the pure pleasure of it!

Tiger Love Positions

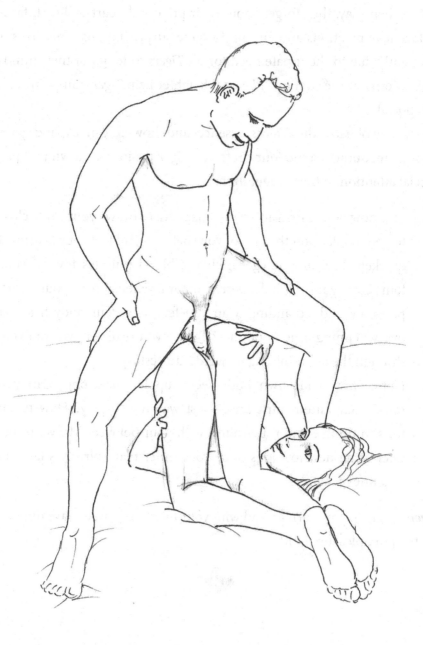

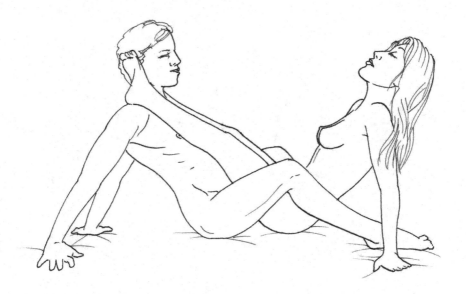

Porcupine Love Positions (Porcairian)

*I*n love positions, *Porcupines* teach others to explore love with a heightened sense of care and sensitivity. They understand their true feelings from the inside out at a deep level. *Porcupines* tend to focus on details and like everything to be perfect.

Quite cautious by nature, *Porcupines* take their time getting close, but once they let you past their formidable defenses, you're sure to find a rare, tender being inside. Sensitive to smell, *Porcupines* don't like perfumes and scents, preferring fresh, clean smells.

Porcupines can teach you to slow down. What's the rush about anyway? Courting a *Porcupine* is like going back in time to an era when things moved more slowly and customs were more refined.

Because *Porcupines* are shy, they gravitate toward gentle, discreet love positions. They almost always prefer to shower or bathe before making love. In fact, some of their favorite positions are realized in the shower or while in water.

Drawn to learning Tantra, *Porcupines* love perfecting their lovemaking skills. This can help them because their bodies are often extremely sensitive. They can get triggered into negative responses (raising their "quills") if they're not touched just right. Through Tantric practice and discipline, *Porcupines* often learn to temper this reaction. Then they find themselves experiencing unusual and even exotic love positions that, through self-mastery, they come to love. This can make navigating those sharp quills an exciting challenge and well worth the effort!

When exploring the *Porcupine's* essence and how it can expand your lovemaking, practice the four preferred *Porcupine* positions shown and pay special attention to these suggestions:

1. Go slowly. Always begin with a shower or swim in a body of water (when possible) before practicing the *Porcupine* love positions. Feel how gentle your touch can be. Start touching lightly, as if your fingers were feathers. Notice how beautiful your *Porcupine* lover's quills are—how if you move slowly and with love, they soften and fold back effortlessly, allowing you in.

2. Foreplay is essential with *Porcupines*. Real porcupines like to lick themselves clean carefully and slowly, especially their hands. Just like their animal totem, *Porcupines* love to use their tongues. They enjoy oral sex as part of their foreplay—and more often than not—as the main course! *Porcupines* can help you learn to slow down and move with care. In Spanish, the perfect word to describe how to make love with a *Porcupine* is *cuidado* (with care).

3. Once a *Porcupine's* formidable defenses are quelled, things can get exciting. *Porcupines* have inner worlds that are exquisitely refined and expansive. If you have reached this inner realm, take your time and savor your well-earned reward! When you do, you'll receive treasures that last a lifetime.

Porcupine Love Positions

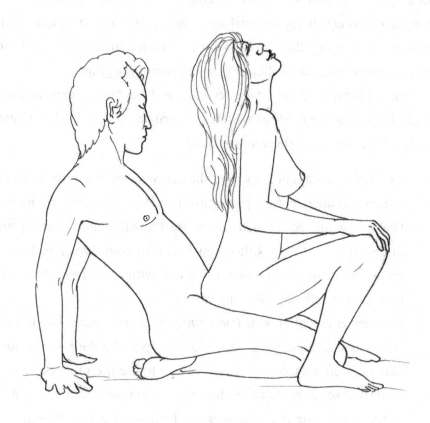

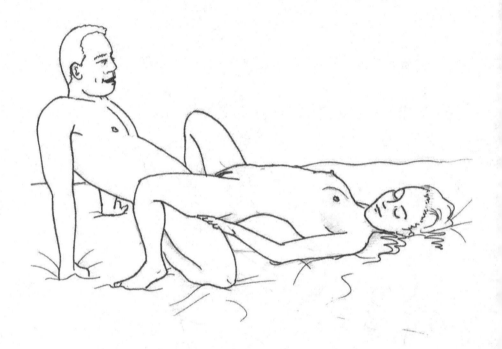

Dolphin Love Positions (Dolphinian)

*T*he *Dolphin's* essence in love positions reflects the art of being playful.

Real dolphins love to play and make love for the pure pleasure of it! In fact, in the animal kingdom, they're the only animal that makes love for enjoyment, not just for procreation.

In their lighthearted way, *Dolphins* bring a special quality to making love. They also embody their animal totem's feeling of being free and can be open to playing with many different lovers. They don't like to take life seriously. When they feel drama coming their way, they may take off before their charged lover's sentence is even finished.

Dolphins are naturally in their bodies and combine strength with flexibility in a wonderfully balanced way. They love to laugh.

When exploring the *Dolphin's* essence in lovemaking, practice the four preferred *Dolphin* positions shown. Pay special attention to how you feel and what energies arise as you follow these suggestions:

1. Allow your natural sexual energy to arise within you. Explore the sensation of being free. Feel the freedom that comes from knowing you are loved and accepted by all of existence, especially your family. Sense how this feeling of total acceptance can melt away tensions you may have carried all your life. Sense how your loved ones are swimming in community with you in this friendly oceanic experience. Know that you have arrived. Welcome home!

2. Sense how your body wants to swim as fast as it can, jump out of the water, and then fly through the air just for the pure joy of being alive. See how you can be attracted to many love partners (even though you may not intend to act your attractions out); feel how you can see the beauty in all of them. Allow your passion to fully awaken! As you play with different *Dolphin* love positions, remember to smile. (As the famous Indian teacher Meher Baba once said, "Be happy; don't worry.") Just the simple act of smiling will activate exciting new places to explore!

3. Feel how your body is naturally buoyant, how every cell in your body is supported by this magical oceanic existence. The natural support of being in the water allows your body to relax. Experience how it naturally leads you into fun, imaginative love positions when you follow your joy in play.

Dolphins have the ability to help you learn how to play and laugh freely. Drop your expectations, your agendas, and smile. Take in your joy of being alive! Feel all the sensations in your body as if you were weightless and gravity had no effect. Sense how being free of gravity feels. What else is possible?

Dolphin Love Positions

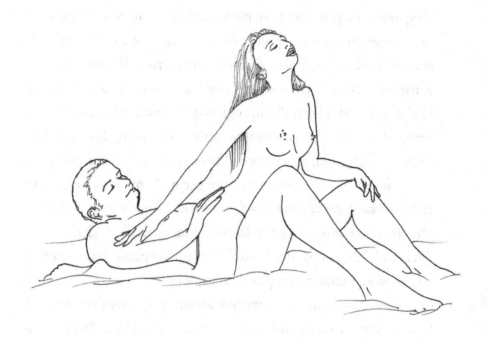

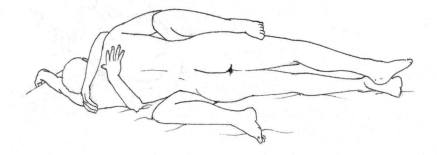

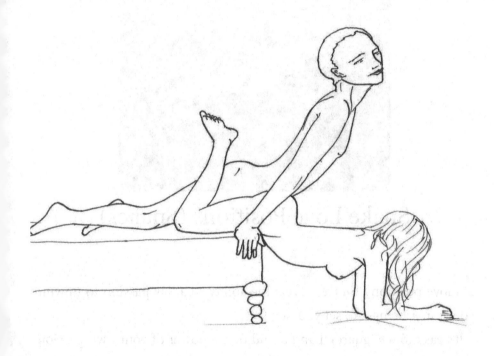

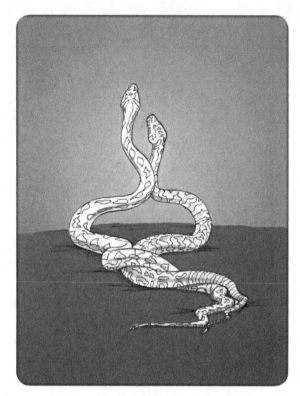

Snake Love Positions (Snakes)

*I*n love positions, *Snakes* reveal the ability to allow passion to unwind your inner being—to set yourself free.

It's easy to feel guarded and afraid of the power of your own passion. What if you get rejected? What if you're too much for your lover? *Snakes* are powerful and supple at the same time, allowing them to roll with whatever happens. They follow their passions and never feel concerned if they're too much! In fact, *Snakes* possess an inner confidence that borders on narcissism. Their bodies—the most flexible of all the animal totems—can easily master a wide variety of love positions.

Snakes tend to be highly strategic, almost calculating. They use their minds to survey each situation before rushing in. Contrary to *Rhinos* who charge right in, *Snakes* take their time, weighing decisions and actions carefully. Once an action is decided, though, watch out. *Snakes* possess incredible animal magnetism. Their powerful passion runs deep, often moving their lovers to their core.

When exploring the *Snake's* essence and how this totem can expand your lovemaking, practice the four preferred *Snake* positions shown and pay special attention to these suggestions:

1. Feel how your natural sexual energy (like Kundalini) can arise within you. Allow your passion to flow freely. Notice how you're not afraid of your shadow side, that you have a full palette of pathways for expressing your love. Feel your power to strike out with force like a rattlesnake. Sense your ability to engulf your lover with your strong body like a boa constrictor. Feel your power to be slow and gentle like a king snake. *Snakes* embody primordial qualities and do not fear power. They hold the secret of life and death inside their ancient knowing.

2. Feel how incredibly flexible your *Snake* body is—how you can assume any shape, any posture, like a master yogi.

3. Pay special attention to your eyes. *Snakes'* eyes are mesmerizing. Once they lock on to something, they never turn away. Under the gaze of a *Snake's* eyes, you can almost feel undressed when you're fully clothed. While practicing the Snake-preferred love positions, notice your own eyes. Can you share the intensity of how you're feeling through these portals to your soul?

A snake's intensity reveals much about being comfortable with who you are and playing as big as you can. Similarly, *Snakes* have the ability to teach you how *not* to shy away from what you sincerely want. *Snakes* play all out, both in the light and in the darkness.

Snake Love Positions

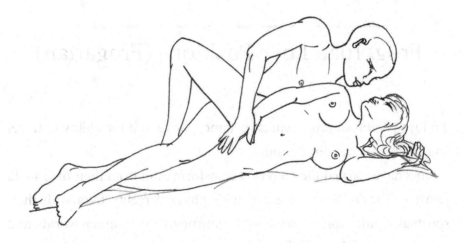

Frog/Toad Love Positions (Frogarian)

*I*n love positions, *Frogs* reflect metamorphosis and the ability to travel spiritually to other dimensions.

Frogs have learned the secrets of transformation from their own soul's journey. They're less concerned with physical reality than with their spiritual connections. They love to journey to new inner worlds and frequently shed their old "skins," continually renewing themselves.

When real frogs search for their mate, they sing their songs loud and clear into the open night. *Frogs* listen for their lover's heart song, paying special attention to how this makes them feel.

Because of their personal mystical qualities, *Frogs* come across as attractive to others. Because they tend to focus on the spiritual qualities of love and the soul's journey, they're not attracted to physically exotic love positions. Hence, their preferred positions may seem deceptively simple. In fact, real frogs do not reproduce through internal fertilization like most animals. The male frog appears to be mounting the female frog engaging in intercourse, but in fact, it's piggybacking on top of her, fertilizing the eggs as they are laid externally. Similarly, *Frogs* are often focused more on the spiritual connection with their lovers than the physical.

When exploring the *Frog's* essence and how it can expand your lovemaking, practice the four preferred *Frog* positions shown and pay special attention to these suggestions:

1. Close your eyes and allow your natural sexual energy to arise within. Let your breath help you relax and deepen your breathing. Make soft sounds with your breathing. With your eyes still closed, let go of your thinking and focus on being present. Now, press your forehead to your lover's (if physically possible; otherwise do it psychically) and allow your electrical energy fields to merge. Shift your attention to the colors you're seeing and play with this energy for a while. Let the colors move and swirl as if forming the origins of dreams and visions. See if you can sense that *you are not your body*; that you *have* a body and, at the same time, you're so much more. Notice how your body gently rocks in rhythm with your lover's in the physical world, swimming between the dimensions of this world and your own rich inner world. How can this awareness expand your reality?

2. Feel how your body loves to "float on the surface of the water" like a frog or just rest gently on a "thin green lily pad." Notice how your legs can relax and stretch out comfortably with the feeling of nowhere to go, nothing to do. Put your attention on your inner journey. Sense your lover floating silently beside you. Realize that the less you move, the more you feel. Deepen into this stillness.

Can you sense the amazement of sharing this point of stillness with your beloved?

Frogs are master Relaxaterians! While exploring the *Frog* love positions, remember to relax . . . and breathe . . . knowing there is nothing to do, nowhere to go. Allow your inner dream world to arise.

Frog/Toad Love Positions

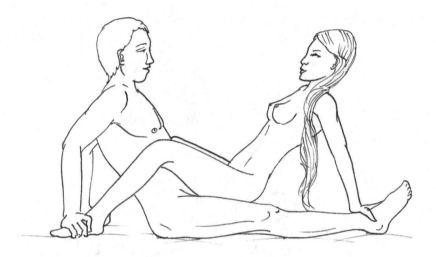

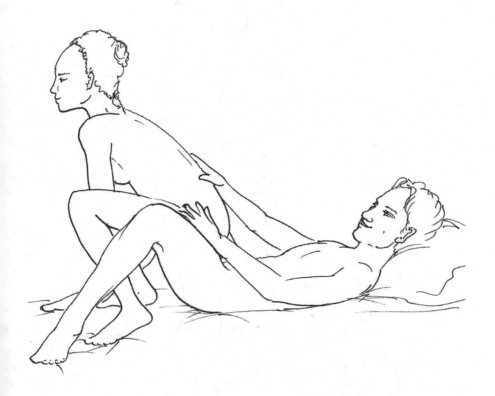

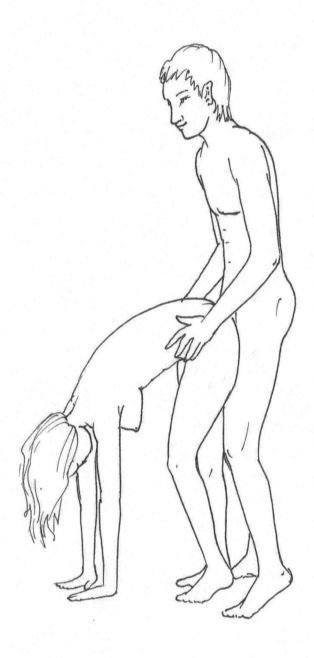

Turtle/Tortoise Love Positions (Terrapin)

Turtles reveal an ability to move slowly and with steadfast determination when evoking their favorite love positions. Indeed, *Turtles* can last for an extremely long time making love while remaining present and focused—their greatest gift.

Loving to acquire knowledge and continually grow, *Turtles* are often keenly interested in the art of making love and are drawn to learning Tantric techniques. They tend to be less concerned with emotions and passion than with mastering their chosen skills.

Turtles are equally at home in water and on land, thus allowing them to remain consistent in many different environments. This trait of moving slowly supports them in merging with a wide variety of totems.

Turtles prefer love positions that allow them to move slowly and feel deeply. Surprisingly flexible, they can enjoy more exotic and challenging lovemaking positions. These appeal to their need to master skills and excel. *Turtles* can be quite competitive, even if it's with themselves.

When exploring the *Turtle's* essence and how it can expand your lovemaking, practice the four preferred *Turtle* love positions shown and pay special attention to these suggestions:

1. First and foremost, slow everything down. Then drop inside yourself even deeper and slow things down another whole notch. Focus on your breath. Find a rhythm you can sustain for a long time. (Remember, the tortoise won the race by being steady and focused.) *Turtles* understand a profound secret—that mastering rhythmic slow breathing is essential in elevated lovemaking.

2. Practice, practice, practice. Explore difficult love positions; master those that aren't easy at first. Remember when you first tried to touch your toes? You may not have been able to get close but by practicing daily for as little as a week, you succeeded. Now apply this principle to mastering new, exotic love positions.

Turtles can help you slow down and feel life deeply. They also have an incredible capacity to stay the course. *Turtles* know a second secret; repetition is not boring, but rather a key to personal evolution and power.

Turtle/Tortoise Love Positions

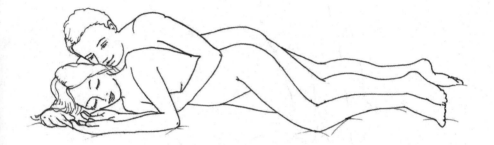

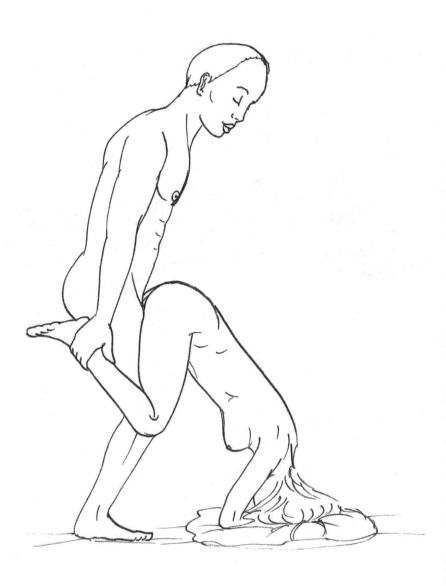

Pheasant/Peacock Love Positions
(Peacoshian)

*F*or *Peacocks*, their essence in love positions can be found in their ability to know and feel how beautiful they truly are.

The *Peacock's* core nature is to love all humanity—not to be confused with being promiscuous. Rather, they possess the quality of agape, or universal unconditional love. Because their totem is a bird, *Peacocks* also have a rather high metabolism. Thus they tend to move faster in lovemaking than many other animal totem types. Have you ever watched birds make love? Everything happens fast.

Peacock kisses are akin to pecks, but what they lack in depth and duration, they compensate for in intensity and frequency. Their lovemaking reflects the nature of their totem, with a bit of strutting around at first, then a speedy embrace ending with an intense climax.

Peacocks tend not to be concerned with romantic love and all the drama that often entails. Instead, they have an eye on the bigger picture. In fact, they have all "100 eyes" of their "tail feathers" seeing every angle, every possibility.

When exploring the *Peacock's* essence and how it can expand your lovemaking, practice the four preferred *Peacock* love positions shown and pay special attention to these suggestions:

1. Feel from within yourself how beautiful you truly are. Allow your natural sexual energy to arise from this place. Explore how you feel being totally desired by your partner. Can you release all ideas that you're not totally desirable? Determine who you would be without your "story."

2. Allow your energy to expand. Feel your heart beating fast like that of a hummingbird. Can you let go of all your preconceived ideas that making love has to be a slow, drawn-out process . . . that you need to perform . . . that you need to satisfy your lover in any way? Feel free to make love quickly, just as birds do, with no apologies, no niceties. Let your energy explode with total freedom and abandonment.

3. Feel the freedom that not being ruled by romantic love can give you. Know that you are part of a grander scheme that embraces love for all humanity.

Peacocks can help you *not* get attached and identified with your lover. They support you in keeping your eye (eyes) on the idea that people are all interconnected—that we are all one.

Pheasant/Peacock Love Positions

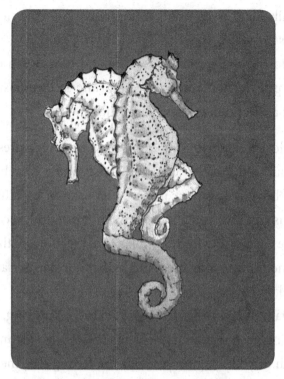

Seahorse Love Positions (Sea-airian)

S*eahorses* reveal how to better attune with your lover. Incredibly intuitive, *Seahorses* blend with their lovers in a way that's wondrous to experience. This quality alone can be enough to heal your soul.

In the ocean, the very survival of seahorses depends on their ability to perfectly synchronize with their partner during egg transfer; otherwise, their precious eggs will be lost to the continuously churning sea. Real seahorses can spend hours and sometimes days attuning with each other—a process called the pre-dawn dance.

Just like their totem, *Seahorses* engage in long foreplay that's not about raising sexual energy but rather about tuning in to their partner. *Seahorses* love to breathe gently together. They enjoy moving slowly in unison, just like dancers in Contact Improvisation—the closest thing to the seahorse's pre-dawn dance that humans can know.

When exploring the *Seahorse's* essence and how it can expand your lovemaking, practice the four preferred *Seahorse* love positions shown and pay special attention to these suggestions:

1. First, close your eyes. Can you feel your lover's presence? Sense how you both breathe. Can you synchronize your breath? Settle in and breathe together, just for the sake of breathing, and see how this can give you a natural high. From this place of stillness, practice each of the four *Seahorse* love positions without moving. Just synchronize your breathing with your partner and feel what you feel.

2. Start again and this time, feel how your lover is moving. Move slowly, mirroring each other's movements, finding a rhythm that works for both of you. No hurry; adopt the feeling that there's nowhere else to go. Have you ever watched synchronized swimming? These swimmers have mastered the art of being *Seahorses*! Just follow the natural rhythm that begins to emerge and experience where life can take you.

3. Can you sense your dream body and the freedom it allows? Living in the ocean, seahorses have a sense of weightlessness. Can you feel how your dream body is weightless? Can you explore new ways to move? In finding new and creative love positions, *Seahorses* often become quite acrobatic.

Seahorses teach you how to unite your dream body with your physical body. In dreamtime, everything is possible!

Seahorse Love Positions

Section V:

Symbols

for

Genital Readings

Symbols for Genital Readings

Each animal totem has its own symbol with these four variations:

- When the symbol is large, it represents the Primary Animal Totem.
- When it's small, it represents a Further Influence Primary Animal Totem.
- When it's large with a circle around it, it represents the Inner Animal Totem.
- When it's small with a circle around it, it represents a Further Influence Inner Animal Totem.

Use these genital reading animal totem symbols as shorthand when writing notes and configuring a reading. Following are the 12 samples:

Outer Symbols		Inner Symbols
⋀	Rhino	
	Elephant	
	Chameleon	
	Possum	
	Tiger	
	Porcupine	
	Dolphin	
	Snake	
	Frog	
	Turtle	
	Peacock	
	Seahorse	

Female Genitals –
Physical Descriptions and Drawings

When describing a woman's genitals, it's helpful to know the meaning of the following terms:

Clitoris: The clitoris is the part of the vagina located at the top of the vaginal opening that's often small and knoblike in appearance. When excited sexually, the clitoris fills with blood much in the same way a man's penis swells with blood. It's often hidden and hard to find under the clitoral hood, which is a smooth-skinned, hood-shaped flap of skin covering the sensitive clitoris. For some women, the clitoris can be quite large and pronounced.

Labia Majora (mounds): The labia majora are the two fleshy mounds located on the outside edge of both sides of the vaginal opening. Sometimes puffy, they often appear like two symmetrical mounds covered with dense hair (unless the hair has been shaved). In genital readings, we refer to the labia majora as "the mounds" for simplicity.

Labia Minora (labia): The labia minora are the smooth-skinned lips that bracket the immediate vaginal opening. These lips can form in many shapes and sizes, giving a unique expression to each of the 12 animal totem types. In genital readings, we refer to these inner lips as the "labia" for short.

Yoni: *Yoni* is another word for vagina.

Positioning: The physical location of the clitoris, mounds, and labia on the female pelvis helps determine which animal archetype is presenting in a genital reading.

Size and Shape: It's important to observe and evaluate the size and shape of the clitoris, mounds, and labia to give an accurate genital reading.

Read each of the following 12 vagina descriptions carefully.

For each of the 12 types of female genitals, three drawings are presented, with each one showing different variations and angles. The drawings, combined with the written descriptions, will assist you in making an accurate genital reading.

Take your time. Many of the differences are subtle and require careful observation. Sometimes more than one animal totem may seem to be presenting. In that case, choose the animal totem with a genital description that's most similar to the subject's genitals as the Primary Totem. If a close second is apparent, its corresponding totem is often associated with the Further Influences part of the reading. To keep it simple, limit the Further Influences to no more than two additional animal totems.

Trust your intuition; your first choice is often the correct one.

Rhino (Female)

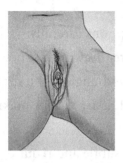  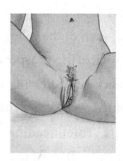

Most defining female *Rhino* characteristic:

Presence of a visibly large clitoris.

The clitoral hood will be large as well. The labia may have a large piece or flap-like protrusion at the top of the yoni. The mounds are average in size. The pelvis tends to have a slanted or pitched-forward posture.

A feeling of masculine assertive energy may be present.

Elephant (Female)

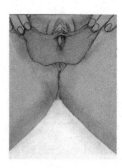

Most defining female *Elephant* characteristic:

Labia lips look like elephant ears when open.

Often heart-shaped in appearance, the labia lips are strikingly large and floppy. The mounds are often small to medium in size while the labia may be dark in color.

A feeling of a big energy field may be present.

Chameleon (Female)

 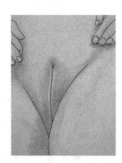 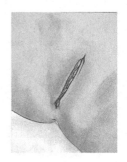

Most defining female *Chameleon* characteristics:

Mounds are flat and labia lips are tight, almost nonexistent.

The entire vagina appears like one long thin slit. A clean, sleek appearance prevails. Skin is sensitive and tends to change color easily. Little or finely textured hair is present.

A feeling of evasiveness may be present.

Possum (Female)

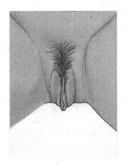  

Most defining female *Possum* characteristic:

Labia lips are pronounced and convoluted.

The way the labia lips naturally hang and curl can appear like a possum hanging upside down. The lips look wrinkly; the hair is wiry or curly. Scraggly looking hair is often dark, but not always. Sometimes a contracted, slumping body posture is apparent.

A feeling of hiding may be present.

Tiger (Female)

Most defining female *Tiger* characteristics:

Presence of beautifully shaped, medium to large plump mounds with little or no labia lips.

The vagina is centrally placed on the pelvis. Fine hair, often shaved. Good blood circulation and coloration. Often hair is light-colored, but not always.

Panther, Jaguar, Cheetah, Cougar, Lion: These variations of the *Tiger* totem are, for the most part, discerned intuitively. The presence of moles helps distinguish the *Cheetah*; the other Big Cats are harder to identify. Once you identify *Tiger* characteristics, use your intuition to sense any variations that may be present.

A feeling of heart-fullness may be present.

Porcupine (Female)

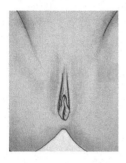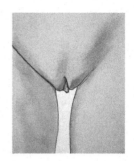

Most defining female *Porcupine* characteristics:

The vagina overall is small and positioned low on the pelvis.

The mounds are also small or flat, with the labia lips being prominent and full. The entire vagina is located almost underneath the pelvis between the legs, facing downward. Wiry, curly hair, often dark in color, is sometimes apparent but not always.

A feeling of cautiousness may be present.

Dolphin (Female)

 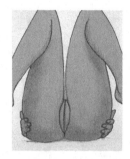 

Most defining female *Dolphin* characteristic:

Presence of beautifully shaped, large, elongated, crescent-shaped mounds.

Matching long curved mounds have wide mid-sections on both sides, almost looking like two dolphins. Small or no labia minora lips often have no hair or fine hair with smooth skin.

A feeling of playfulness may be present.

Snake (Female)

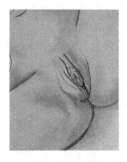  

Most defining female *Snake* characteristics:

Vagina is very long; labia lips are convoluted, frequently in an s-shaped folding pattern.

The two irregular labia lips do not mirror each other. The mounds are often medium to flat in size and are long and thin.

Rattlesnake, Boa Constrictor, and ***King Snake*** are all variations that can be discerned by instinct. Once you identify the *Snake* Totem, use your intuition to sense if variations might be presenting.

Feelings of mystery and danger may be present.

Frog (Female)

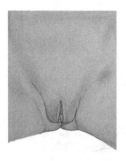  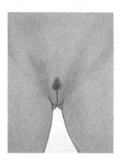

Most defining female *Frog* characteristics:

Vagina is small in overall size; mounds are very plump with almost no labia minora lips present.

The placement of the mounds is low under the pelvis, with the vagina almost facing downward. Warts may be evident.

Feelings of merriment and contentment may be present.

Turtle (Female)

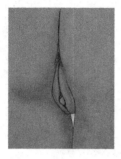  

Most defining female *Turtle* characteristic:

When viewing the vagina with legs closed, it looks like a turtle in its shell with its head sticking out in the middle.

The mounds tend to be full, with the labia minora lips having a bigger flap in the middle than others.

A feeling of inner strength may be present.

Peacock (Female)

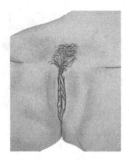

Most defining female *Peacock* characteristic:

The appearance of balance is present in the vagina.

The mounds are symmetrical and average size, the labia lips are proportional, and the vagina placement is centrally placed on the pelvis. The manicure and adornment of the vagina is given special attention, with the hair sometimes shaved in a fanlike pattern, resembling a peacock's tail feathers. Piercing and jewelry are frequently seen (although these can be observed in other types, too).

A feeling of "look at me; I am so beautiful" may be present.

Seahorse (Female)

Most defining female *Seahorse* characteristic:

Labia lips have matching shapes on both sides of the vagina like a mirroring quality.

The labia minora lips may even have a seahorse shape and appearance. Look for a curlicue shape at the bottom of the labia lips. The mounds are less prominent than in other totems. Often the vagina has a fragile look. It's often medium in size, with thin hair that's frequently dark but can be any color.

A feeling of warmth and caring may be present.

Female Genital Map Determining Which Animal Totem is Presenting

Let's get started. First, review all 12 sets (3-pictures each) of the 12 different female genital types. Take your time and read each corresponding description carefully. Identifying the 12 totem types may be confusing at first, but in time it will become easy. Here are some pointers that will help you. Remember that most genitals will present a few of the different animal totem key features. Your task is to determine the most prominent feature which in turn will determine the Primary Animal Totem associated with the subject's genitals. Any close runner-up features can be used to identify the "Further Influences".

Here are some key questions to help you navigate the 12 different female genital types:

Does the subject present a very large clitoris? If so, she is a *Rhino*.

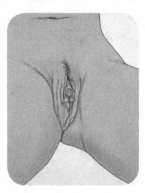

Rhino

Does the subject present very large labia minora (lips) that easily open-up and look like elephant ears? If so she is an *Elephant*.

Elephant

Does the subject present no labia minora (lips) and no labia majora (mounds)? Does the vagina appear almost like a slit? If so, she is a *Chameleon*.

Chameleon

Does the subject present obvious labia majora (mounds) but little or no labia minora (lips)? A few choices begin with this configuration.

Look closer now. Are the labia majora (mounds) rather plump and located centrally on the torso...front and center when your subject is standing? Make sure there is not a labia minora (lip) piece protruding out from in between the mounds in the middle as this can indicate she may be a *Turtle*.

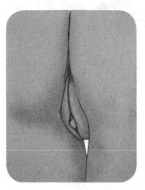

Turtle

Are the mounds rather short and puffy? If so, then she is a *Tiger*.

Tiger

Look closer again. Are the labia majora (mounds) still centrally placed on the torso but differing from the *Tiger* mounds by exhibiting a significant narrowing at the ends, making the mounds appear like the shape of 2 dolphins pressed up next to each other? If so, then she is a *Dolphin*.

Dolphin

Look closer again. Are the labia majora (mounds) rather small and placed lower down on the torso, almost between the legs facing downward, rather than facing forward? Are there almost no labia minora (lips) present? If so, then she is a *Frog*.

Frog

Look closer still. Are the labia major (mounds) still pronounced, but now a small flap of labia minora (lip) can be seen protruding from in-between the middle section of the mounds, appearing almost like a turtle sticking its head out form its shell? If so, then she is a *Turtle*.

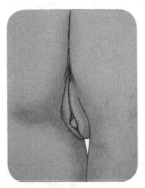

Turtle

Does the subject present labia minora (lips) but no labia major (mounds)? A few choices begin with this configuration.

Again, if the labia minora (lips) are very large and centrally placed on the torso, then she is an *Elephant*.

Elephant

Look closer. Are the labia minora (lips) clearly present but rather small? Are they placed low down on the torso almost between the subject's legs, facing downward? If so, she is a *Porcupine*.

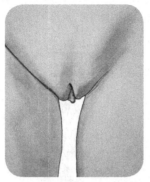

Porcupine

Does the subject present no pronounced labia major (mounds) and no significant labia minora (lips), but more than just a slit?

Look closer. Does the subject present some mounds and lips? Look even closer now at the inner configuration of the labia minora (lips). Is the opening very long and are the inner lips very convoluted, with no symmetrical pattern? Then she is a *Snake*.

Snake

Look closer. Does the subject still present some mounds and lips? Look even closer now, is the vagina opening small to medium in size? Are the inner lips symmetrical, matching on each side? If so then she is a *Seahorse*.

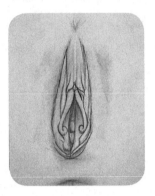

Seahorse

Look closer again. Are the labia majora (mounds) more pronounced than the labia minora (lips). Is there wiry hair present? The inner lips are very important in this determination. Are the inner lips convoluted and not symmetrical? Is the vagina opening medium to big, but not very long? If so, then she is a *Possum*.

Possum

Look very close now. Are there any piercings present? Look closely at the hair trimming style. Is the vagina carefully shaved, but leaving a fan of hair above the vagina opening? Are the labia majora (mounds) and labia minora (lips) subtle yet visible? Is there a sense of beauty and elegance present? If so, then she is a *Peacock*.

Peacock

Male Genitals – Physical Descriptions and Drawings

When describing a man's penis, it's helpful to know the meaning of the following terms:

Shaft: The shaft of the penis is the elongated cylindrically shaped middle section of the penis. It is the part between the balls and the head (tip).

Head: The head of the penis is the section at the tip of the shaft.

Balls: The balls are the sacks hanging down at the base of the shaft of the penis.

Size and Shape: The size and shape of the shaft, head, and balls are important to evaluate to give an accurate genital reading. The shape of the shaft can be straight, curved, or even crooked.

Angle of Erection: The actual angle of an erection can determine which animal totem is presenting. This angle can vary from almost straight up at 180 degrees to hanging straight down.

Tilt: When the penis is fully erect, it's important to view the subject from straight on to determine if the penis leans to the left or right or if it goes straight up. This observation is especially important in determining which animal totem is presenting. Also, viewing the penis from the side helps determine if the shaft is curved in a crescent moon shape.

Texture: When giving a genital reading, observe the condition of the skin on the shaft of the penis. Is it rough or smooth? Does it have raised veins? Are moles present?

For each of the 12 types of male genitals, three drawings are presented, with each one showing different variations and angles. The drawings, combined with the written descriptions, will assist you in making an accurate genital reading.

Take your time. Many of the differences are subtle and require careful observation. Sometimes more than one animal totem may seem to be presenting. In that case, choose the animal totem with a genital description that's most similar to the subject's genitals as the Primary Totem. If a close second is apparent, its corresponding totem is often associated with the Further Influences part of the reading. To keep it simple, limit the Further Influences to no more than two additional animal totems.

Trust your intuition; your first choice is often the correct one.

Rhino (Male)

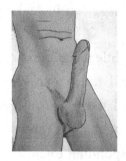 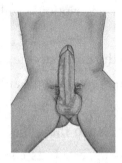 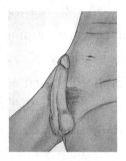

Most defining male *Rhino* characteristic:

The presence of a visibly large, fat penis with a small head.

The head of the penis is smaller in diameter than the shaft. The angle of erection is straight up. It might have a slight curve. The pelvis is often tilted forward as if thrusting or charging.

A feeling of over-confidence is often present.

Elephant (Male)

 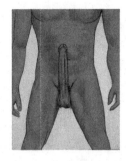 

Most defining male *Elephant* characteristic:

The presence of a visibly giant penis, especially when flaccid.

Large hanging balls (goes with a big overall body, feet, and hands). The erect penis has a straight-up angle and is usually quite impressive. Its texture is frequently rough, almost earthy in nature.

A feeling of being drawn in may be present.

Chameleon (Male)

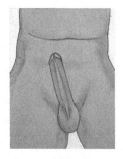 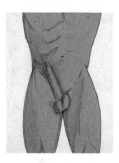 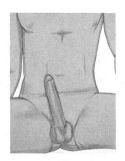

Most defining male *Chameleon* characteristic:

The erect penis often tilts right (as seen from the subject's view).

Often the penis is thin; sometimes it displays a different coloration than the body. The texture is usually smooth but dry. The shaft and head have the same diameter. Frequently, small tight balls are observed.

A feeling of versatility may be present.

Possum (Male)

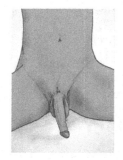 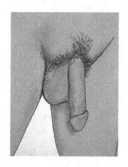 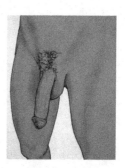

Most defining male *Possum* characteristic:

The penis tends to be limp even when trying to be erect.

It can become erect, but this requires much effort. It's often small in size, although size can vary greatly. Wiry, scraggly hair is often dark. When flaccid, the penis has a look of a possum hanging upside down.

A feeling of wanting to hide may be present.

Tiger (Male)

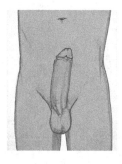 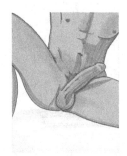 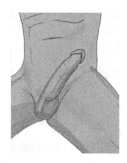

Most defining male *Tiger* characteristic:

The erect penis often tilts left (as seen from the subject's view).

It's usually plump, thick, and above average in size, while the balls are medium in size. The hair is often light colored but not always. The erection has a bouncy, springy quality.

Check to see if any moles on the shaft of the penis are present or helpful hints to identify the other Big Cat characteristics.

Panther, Jaguar, Cheetah, Cougar, Lion (variations of the *Tiger* totem) can be discerned intuitively. The presence of moles helps distinguish the *Cheetah*, while the other Big Cats are harder to identify. Use your intuition to sense any other variations.

A friendly feeling may be present.

Porcupine (Male)

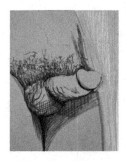  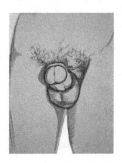

Most defining male *Porcupine* characteristic:

The erect penis is short, stocky, and pudgy looking.

It's small in size with no enlarged head. It usually has bristly looking hair at the base of it and often presents round plump balls that might appear as one fused ball. A light-colored underside is sometimes apparent.

A feeling of guardedness may be present.

Dolphin (Male)

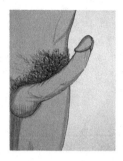 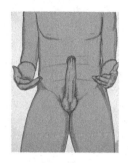 

Most defining male *Dolphin* characteristic:

The erect penis displays a crescent-shaped curve.

The shaft tends to be long, curved, and thin. It has smooth skin and tight, small balls and fine hair at its base. The penis sometimes displays a pink blush.

A feeling of "let's play" may be present.

Snake (Male)

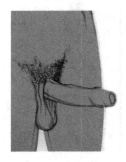  

Most defining male *Snake* characteristics:

The penis tends to be long.

When erect, it's straight up at first, then tends to dip down to a 90-degree angle (pointing straight out) after a short while. Sometimes the shaft is crooked or bent, almost appearing like a snake. The shaft and head of the penis are uniform in thickness and usually smooth skinned.

(Note: The *Snake* is the hardest totem to distinguish because the penis often remains in a straight-up erection, not dropping to the characteristic 90-degree angle. Perhaps it's the *Snake's* secretive nature that makes this totem difficult to figure out. Look at the subject's eyes if you can. For *Snakes*, the eyes will be intense and rarely look away. Rely on your intuition heavily and trust your feelings.)

The ***Rattlesnake, Boa Constrictor,*** and ***King Snake*** are variations of this totem and are discerned intuitively. Once the *Snake* totem has been identified, use your intuition to sense if any variations are also presenting.

An exciting, dangerous feeling may be present.

Frog (Male)

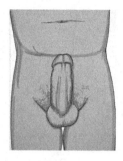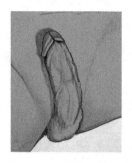

Most defining male *Frog* characteristic:

The erect penis is short, stout, and often has enlarged raised veins.

When erect, it has a straight-up angle. It often has a cubby appearance and warts might be visible on the shaft. The skin tends to be rough and the hair usually wiry and curly.

Feelings of mysticism and adventure may be present.

Turtle (Male)

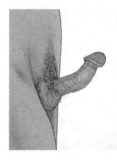 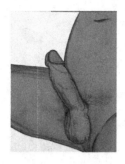 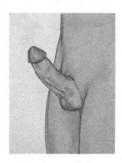

Most defining male *Turtle* characteristic:

The erect penis tends to be short and stout with a big head.

Often the erection angle is 130 degrees (¾ slant) and the shaft might have a slight bent or curved look. The hair can vary. Often the balls are large, especially compared with the shaft size. Sometimes they appear fused like they're one large ball.

A feeling of inner strength may be present.

Peacock (Male)

Most defining male *Peacock* characteristic:

The erect penis tends to be long and thin with an elegantly defined head.

The head has a similar thickness as the shaft. A fuzzy nest of hair is usually present. The balls are usually medium in size. Often the erection angle is 130 degrees (¾ slant). This slant might parallel a pheasant's angle of trajectory when taking off in flight.

A feeling of elegance may be present.

Seahorse (Male)

  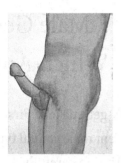

Most defining male *Seahorse* characteristic:

Erect penis displays a distinctly large head although the penis is often small and thin.

There is no curve in the erect penis. The erection can be straight up or at a 130-degree angle (¾ slant). Sometimes the shaft will have ring-like bands. The balls sometimes have a fused appearance as if they were one ball. The small balls often have fine hair.

(Note: *Turtles* and *Seahorses* have similar-looking penises. The key difference is in thickness. *Seahorses* tend to have thin-shafted penises while *Turtles* have stout-shafted penises.)

A feeling of sensitivity may be present.

Male Genital Map Determining Which Animal Totem is Presenting

Let's get started. First, review all 12 sets (3-pictures each) of the 12 different male genital types. Take your time and read each corresponding description carefully. Identifying the 12 totem types may be confusing at first, but in time it will become easy. Here are some pointers that will help you. Remember that most genitals will present a few of the different animal totem key features. Your task is to determine the most prominent feature which in turn will determine the Primary Animal Totem associated with the subject's genitals. Any close runner up features can be used to identify the "Further Influences".

Here are some key questions to help you navigate the 12 different male genital types:

Is the penis very large, even when flaccid? If so, then he is an *Elephant*.

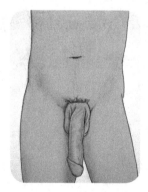

Elephant

Does the subject have a difficult time getting an erection? If so, then he is a *Possum*.

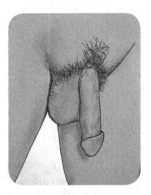

Possum

(Remember to account for the age of the subject…if the male is over 55 years of age, than erection functionality may be more an issue of age rather than totem type.)

When the penis is erect, which way does it lean? If the penis leans to the left (from the subjects point of view looking out), then he is a *Tiger*.

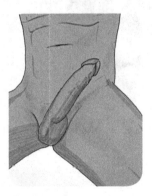

Tiger

If the penis leans to the right (from the subjects point of view looking out), then he is a *Chameleon.*

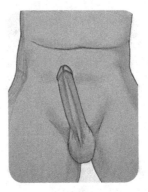

Chameleon

Does the erect penis display a clear crescent-moon shape curve? If so, then he is a *Dolphin.*

Dolphin

When the penis is erect, is it rather big to medium in size tending to be thick in girth? Look closer now, is the head of the penis smaller in diameter than the shaft of the penis? Just like the shape of a rhino's horn. If so, then he is a *Rhino*.

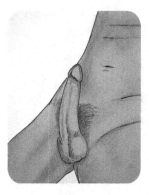

Rhino

(You may note a slight curve in the erect penis, but not as pronounced as with Dolphins.)

When the penis is erect, does it have a 70 degree angle; ¾ of the straight-up angle most erect penises exhibit? Is the penis smooth, with an elegant look to it? Does the head of the penis have a slight hood like shape? If so, then he is a *Peacock*.

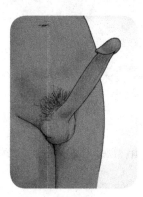

Peacock

Does the erect penis have a crooked or bent shape? Does the penis after being erect a short time drop to a 45 degree angle (sticking out straight forward, rather than up? Is there a secretive feeling present? If so, then he is a *Snake*.

Snake

Does the erect penis exhibit clearly raised veins along the shaft? If so, then he is a *Frog*.

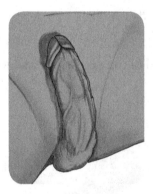

Frog

Is the erect penis smaller in size? If so, then a few possibilities need to be looked at closer.

Is the penis fat? Is wiry hair present? Does the penis have a pudgy kind of look? If so, then he is a *Porcupine.*

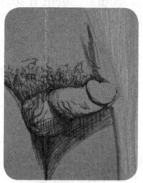

Porcupine

Is the penis shaft very thin with a clearly bigger head? Is the shaft of the penis straight? If so, then he is a *Seahorse.*

Seahorse

Is the shaft of the penis slightly curved? Is the head slightly bigger than the shaft, with a hood like appearance? Does the penis have the look of a turtle sticking its head out from its shell? If so, then he is a *Turtle*.

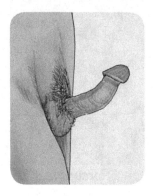

Turtle

Note that the *Seahorse* and *Turtle* totem penis shapes are similar. The main difference is that the *Turtle* totem penis often has a curved shaft and is thicker in girth than the *Seahorse*.

Questionnaire Form - Directions

Answer all 21 questions by circling one choice provided for each question. If more than one answer feels absolutely necessary, pick a second option; but, when possible, choose only one answer for best results. Next, rate the strength of each chosen attribute on a scale of one to five, with five representing the strongest and one representing the weakest.

If you are using the online version of this questionnaire, once you've completed answering the 21 questions and rating the strength of the attributes you've selected, the computer will automatically determine both your primary and secondary Inner Animal Totems.

If you are using the printed questionnaire, you must familiarize yourself with all 12 Inner Animal Totems and the qualities associated with them. Then you will be able to make your own educated determination of your primary and secondary Inner Animal Totems.

If you are new at this, it's a good idea to rely on the online Questionnaire found on the www.SignsOfIntimacy.com Website. As a last resort, if you don't have on-line access, you can simply use your own (or the subject's) birth-date to make a determination of the Inner Animal Totem. (Please refer to "Astrological Correlations to Animal Totems" found in the beginning section of this book in order to utilize birth-dates.)

The Inner Animal Totem Questionnaire

(Choose one answer for each of the 21 questions and rate the degree of strength on a scale of 1 to 5.)

1. How would you describe your underlying emotional state?
Moody
Happy
Friendly
Jovial

2. What is your leadership style?
Leader
Follower
Independent

3. What is your orientation towards yourself?
Mystical
Transformational
Confident, Secure
Insecure

4. How tightly wired are you?
Relaxed
Anxious
Patient
Impatient

5. What is your orientation towards groups?
(Seeks) Center
(Prefers) Background
Loner
Variable

6. What is your orientation towards others?
Nurturing
Self-centered
Lacking Sensitivity

7. How do you connect with other people?
Merge Easily
(Draw others) Close
(Keep others) Distant

8. What is your style when taking action?
Decisive
Indecisive
Impulsive
Careful

9. You have a preference for _____?
Staying home
Traveling
Healthy mix of both

10. How open are you in showing how you feel?
Transparent
Opaque
Honest, Open
Secretive

11. How do you deal with fear?
Fearful
Fearless
Quick to anger, then let go
Furious if Provoked

12. How would you describe your basic attitude?
Playful
Serious
Practical
Idealistic

13. How constant are you with yourself?
Steady
Changeable
Unpredictable

14. How constant are you with others?
Loyal
Fickle
Reliable
Evasive

15. Which best describes the way you process information?
Analytical
Emotional
Mental
Creative

16. How would you describe the vibratory quality of your energy?
Passionate
Enthusiastic
Magnetic
Sensuous

17. How would you describe the vibratory quality of your emotions?
Sensitive
Insensitive or dense
Optimistic
Pessimistic

18. Which best describes your coping style?
Dogmatic
Hedonistic
Controlling
Goal-oriented

19. Which best describes your personality style?
Competitive
Takes risks
Kind
Compassionate, accepting

20. You find yourself often seeking _____?
Novelty
Adventures
Peace
Wisdom

21. You view life form which perspective?
Unique, different, rebellious
Conventional
Spiritual

Section VI:

Animal Reference

Facts

Animal Reference Facts

This reference section is not usually used directly in giving a genital reading but will help you in creating in-depth readings. It provides additional descriptions of physical qualities, behaviors, habitats, and common myths regarding the different animal totems and their corresponding actual animals. Many of the qualities and behaviors found in the animal totems directly relate to their counterparts in the animal kingdom.

Take time to study the 12 animals thoroughly. This background information provides an invaluable source of inspiration for creating fun, insightful readings.

Rhinos

The word *rhinoceros* comes from ancient Greek and literally means "horned nose." Long a symbol of masculine energy, the rhinoceros exudes a sense of raw power, sexual potency, and danger. These animals can be extremely aggressive but only when provoked. Otherwise, they tend to be peaceful by nature and like to roam and graze in their natural habitats.

Rhino Physical Characteristics

This primitive-looking animal dates back millions of years to the Miocene era. The second largest land mammal, the rhinoceros species is smaller than the elephant alone. Its life span is generally 35 to 40 years.

Although rhinos have keen senses of smell and hearing, they have poor eyesight, often causing them to charge without apparent provocation. This tendency can make them seem ill tempered.

Rhinos have rough and exceedingly tough skin that takes considerable force to penetrate. Their thick skin provides a great first line of defense, making it difficult for predators such as lions to bite and harm them effectively.

Some species of rhinoceros have one central horn affixed to their foreheads while others have two horns, one shorter than the other and both centrally placed. These horns make excellent weapons. When provoked, a rhino will tip its head downward and charge—horn (or horns) first—to pierce its adversary.

Rhino Habits

Rhinos are vegetarians and like to be both solitary and in social groups, depending on the species as well as the individual rhino's mood.

Anything but quiet, rhinos grunt, squeak, growl, snort, and bellow. When attacking, the rhino lowers its head, snorts, then charges. Even though it's large and bulky, the rhino is amazingly agile and can turn quickly in a small radius. When charging, it can reach speeds of up to 30 miles an hour!

Rhinos and Mankind

Since 1970, the global rhino population has declined by 90 percent, with only five species remaining in the world today. All have been ruthlessly hunted to the point of extinction or near extinction.

Humans kill rhinos for their horns. The horns of a rhinoceros are made of keratin—the same type of protein that makes up hair and fingernails—not from bone as many people believe.

In the Middle East, particularly in Yemen, rhinoceros horns continue to be coveted by Muslim men, even though imports were banned in 1982. The horn is still used today for the handles of curved daggers called jambiya, which are presented to Yemeni boys at the age of 12. Jambiya are seen as a symbol of manhood and devotion to the Muslim religion. Yemeni men place great value on the rhino dagger handles, used for personal defense and often decorated with jewels.

Along with this tradition, it's thought that rhino horns could help detect the presence of poison. That's why having a dagger handle made of rhino horn was highly desirable. As it turns out, science actually supports this theory. Why? Many poisons are strongly alkaline and tend to react chemically, bubbling when they contact the keratin protein of rhino horn. Thus if poison were present, the bubbling provided a warning sign when the rhino horn handle was placed in the substance being tested. Although handles probably aren't used that way anymore, the whole idea adds to the mystique and value of the horn.

An interesting footnote: Unlike bone, rhinoceros horns become more lustrous and translucent as they age. Thus the older the horns, the more valuable and highly prized they are for making jambiya handles.

In addition to the jambiya practice in Yemen, the Chinese use the rhino horn as medicine (also contributing to the rhino's near extinction). Although it's believed that powdered rhinoceros horn is used as an aphrodisiac in traditional Chinese medicine, this isn't true. Rather, it's prescribed and prized as a remedy for fevers and convulsions.

Rhino Sexuality/Reproduction

Rhinoceros have what's known as an overlap promiscuity mating system. That means female rhinos do not require males to help raise their young; consequently, males frequently have many different mates, especially if they are a dominant male. After three-and-a-half years, a female rhinoceros mates again, often with a different male. The babies remain with their mother for those three-and-a-half years to be protected.

During courtship, male rhinos can become possessive and will fight with other males to gain the favor of a female rhinoceros in estrus (in heat). Estrus often lasts for seven days. During that time, the female rhinoceros sprays scented urine around common areas (such as watering holes) to attract males. When a male rhinoceros smells this potent urine, it urinates on top of the female rhinoceros's urine to cover up the estrus scent. After mating, the male rhinoceros often spends a few more days with the female to ensure the bloodline.

Rhinos in Myths and Stories

In Malaysia, India, and Burma, legends persist about rhinoceroses stamping out forest fires. It's believed that rhinos appear when a fire is lit and come running from the forest to stamp it out. Although no confirmations of this phenomenon exist, the film *The Gods Must Be Crazy* reinforced this ancient myth. In the film, an African rhinoceros stamps out campfires on two separate occasions. The myth that the rhino imparts virility based on its characteristics has led to traditions that have, in fact, helped destroy this ancient and powerful creature.

Rhinos have survived for centuries and represent nature's ability to endure. However, even with their long track record, the risk of the species becoming extinct has greatly accelerated in the last few decades.

Elephants

The word elephant has its origins in the Greek ἐλέφας, meaning "ivory" or "elephant."

Elephants are the largest land mammals on the planet. The African Elephant (Loxodonta Africana) and the Asian/Indian Elephant (Elephas maximus) are the two remaining species alive. The larger of the two, the African Elephant, has ears almost twice the size of an Asian/Indian *Elephant's* ears, which is the easiest way to distinguish between them.

Elephant Physical Characteristics

An elephant can live for 60 to 70 years—a long time in the animal kingdom!

Although their eyesight is relatively poor, elephants have an exceptional sense of hearing and smell. Located not only in their ears but in their trunks, their hearing receptors are sensitive to vibrations—most significantly, the sound of feet hitting the ground. The nerve receptors in their trunks can detect low-frequency sounds exceptionally well. Elephants have been observed putting their trunks on the ground and listening intently. Reportedly, they can hear the footsteps of others in their herd up to five miles away. This ability to communicate through ground vibrations clearly affects an elephant's ability to socialize.

Prized for their large tusks made of ivory, elephants have been hunted for centuries. In South Africa, the elephant population more than doubled—from 8,000 to more than 20,000—in the 13 years after a 1995 South African ban on trade in elephant ivory. In February 2008, this ban was lifted, which has re-stimulated investigations by environmental groups.

Elephants are sometimes called pachyderms (from their original scientific classification), which means thick-skinned animals. And for good reason; an elephant's skin measures 2.5 centimeters (1 in) in thickness.

Its flexible, muscular trunk both combines and elongates its nose and upper lip. This essential body part performs a variety of functions, including feeding, smelling, drinking, hearing, touching, and grasping. The tip of the trunk has a finger-like projection, which helps the elephant grasp small objects. Sensitive enough to pluck a single leaf off a bush, an elephant's trunk is also strong enough to rip a small tree right out of the ground.

Elephant Habits

Elephants are herbivores, eating only plants. Because of their huge size, they need to eat copious amounts of vegetation and have plenty of territory to roam. Simply to survive, an elephant must eat an average of 140 kilograms (300 pounds) of vegetation every day.

Elephants are famous for their trumpet calls, which they make by blowing a rush of air through their nostrils, usually when they get excited.

Generally friendly in nature, elephants often form family groups consisting of one of the elder females as matriarch and three or four related females along with their young offspring. Males are usually solitary but visit female family groups when looking for females in estrus (in heat). Several interrelated family groups can inhabit the same area and know each other well. When they meet at watering holes and feeding places, they greet each other amiably. As social animals, elephants frequently touch and caress one another, entwining their trunks.

Around the age of 14, the mature male leaves his natal group for good. While males live primarily solitary lives, they sometimes form loose associations with other males. These groups are called bachelor herds. In contrast, female elephants tend to live in groups and participate in social activities, especially those pertaining to protecting their offspring.

Females prefer to mate with males that are bigger, stronger, and older than the others, a reproductive strategy that tends to increase their offspring's survival rate.

In ancient India, treatises were written about the care and management of elephants. Over the last few centuries, elephants have become even more important in Indian life and culture. Specialized skills have evolved in capturing, taming, and training elephants.

The symbol of wisdom in Asian cultures, elephants are celebrated for their memory and intelligence. Historians, poets, biologists, and even philosophers have marveled at the elephant, equating it with strength, greatness, and dignity—personifying both divine and human qualities. Possessing huge brains, elephants are endowed with an intelligence rarely found in other animals.

It also appears that elephants have a sense of compassion. They show concern for other family members, take care of weak or injured members of their herd, and seem to grieve over their dead companions. They appear to be fascinated with the bones of dead elephants and actively examine them with their trunks. The myth that elephants carry these bones to secret "elephant burial grounds," however, has no basis in fact.

Elephant Reproduction/Sexuality

Female elephants are only fertile for a couple of days a year. During this time of estrus, male elephants become highly competitive in their efforts to get the attention of the female. Dominant males, often with the largest tusks, usually win the female's attention. This selective process helps ensure the survival of the offspring. Courtship lasts for approximately half an hour with much head rubbing and trunk caressing. Due to odd genital placement, copulation can sometimes be difficult, but mating elephants usually overcome this obstacle. A pregnancy lasts for 22 months and the mother gives birth to a calf. It typically weighs about 115 kilograms (250 pounds) and stands more than 75 centimeters (2.5 feet) tall. Between 12 and 15 years pass before elephants reach sexual maturity. They usually live in the herd with their mothers throughout this period.

Elephants do not mate for life. In fact, females often choose new mates at the time of their next estrus. Overall, elephants tend to be affectionate and display their affection with members of their own gender as well as the opposite sex.

Elephants in Myths and Stories

In the famous Indian folktale *The Elephant and the Blind Men*, each blind man touches a different part of the elephant and perceives it as being akin to that part only. For one, the elephant is like a wall; for another a rope; for a third a tree trunk; and for yet another, a fan. Thus this universal teaching shows that "perceived" reality is only a part of the true picture, not the whole.

Ganesha, the popular Hindu god of wisdom, has a human body and an elephant's head. Lord Ganesha is worshipped daily by millions of people in India. Besides wisdom, this god represents the shattering of obstacles, financial abundance, and good fortune.

Hindus consider their live temple elephants to be embodiments of Lord Ganesha. Devotees receive blessings in the form of a trunk-pat on the head. Temple elephants are held in such high esteem, they even receive a proper Hindu cremation after they die.

As gentle giants of the animal kingdom and harbingers of good luck, elephants are universally treasured.

Chameleons

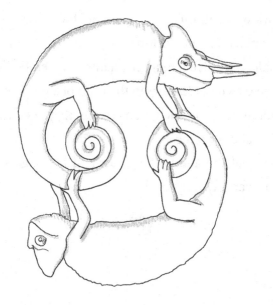

The English word *chameleon* is derived from Latin and the ancient Greek word χαμαιλέων (khamaileon), translating to "ground lion."

Chameleons probably originated in Madagascar, which is home to almost half of all the 150 known species today. The remaining species live in India, Sri Lanka, the Middle East, southern Europe, and northern Africa. Chameleons have also been introduced to parts of the United States, including California, Florida, and Hawaii.

When people think of chameleons, they often think of lizards that can change color to blend in with their surroundings. However, their ability to change color is only one of many interesting qualities unique to chameleons. They have evolved with specialized characteristics that set them apart in the lizard world.

Chameleon Physical Characteristics

Chameleons have feet that are more like a parrot's feet than like those of other reptiles. Termed zygodactyl, the feet have two pincer-like "fingers" sticking out toward the rear and two toward the front on each foot. This makes it easy for them to hold on to branches, which is where they spend most of their lifespan. Many chameleons have prehensile tails and, like monkeys, can wrap their tails around branches to hold on. This allows them to be highly mobile, although not all chameleons have this type of tail.

Chameleons have exceedingly long tongues to use in hunting. At the end of their tongues is a type of suction cup covered in thick mucus that helps them capture their prey. Most chameleon species have a tongue that's nearly as long as their entire body; some have tongues that are twice as long as their bodies.

When a chameleon is capturing prey, its tongue strikes out faster than the human eye can see. The suction cup at the tip hits its target in about 30 thousandths of a second. Once the cup sticks to the prey, the chameleon immediately draws its "catch" back into its mouth and consumes it.

In another distinctive feature, chameleons can move their eyes separately, allowing them to focus independently. Their eyes can also swivel 360 degrees so they can see in all directions without moving their bodies.

Chameleons are able to change the color of their bodies due to specialized cells that contain pigments as well as other cells that reflect color from light. These amazing cells react to the chameleon's mood, the temperature of its environment, and the amount of light available.

Contrary to popular belief, chameleons can't change their color at will to match their surroundings. However, different chameleon species are able to change different colors, which can include pink, blue, red, orange, green, black, brown, light blue, yellow, and turquoise. Because they're relatively slow-moving creatures, their color-changing protective mechanism greatly benefits them in their quest for survival. However, chameleon color changes relate more to communication and air temperature reaction than hiding and camouflage. For example, males change to bright, intense colors to demonstrate their dominance over other males; females change coloration to show they're receptive to mating.

Chameleon species vary greatly in length from 1.3 inches to 27 inches. Different species have different body shapes, with many species being sexually dimorphic. The males typically have more ornate features than females, such as brighter colors and pronounced ornamental bony structures. Although chameleons generally eat other insects, larger chameleons have been known to eat small animals and other lizards. A few species, such as Jackson's Chameleon (C. jacksonii) and the Veiled Chameleon (C. calyptratus) eat small amounts of plant vegetation as well.

Chameleon Reproduction/Sexuality

Being reptiles, chameleons are cold blooded and need the warmth of the sun to get their blood flowing. Female chameleons lay eggs by first digging a nest in the earth. Male chameleons can become quite aggressive around females during mating. The male will puff out its chest and display its brightest colors. It will fight other males to have the privilege of fertilizing the female's eggs. After a short-lived courtship and fertilization, the female and male chameleon will part ways. When the young hatch, they are born alone and need to fend for themselves immediately.

Chameleons in Myths and Stories

The Bantu of South Africa have a legend about the chameleon that explains how death came into this world. One day, God (Unkulunkulu) sent a chameleon (lunwaba) to tell the people, "Man shall not die." Well, the chameleon moseyed forth, stopping to eat along the way. After a while, Unkulunkulu sent a second messenger, a lizard—the blue-headed gecko (intulo). The gecko traveled faster than the slow chameleon and made great time. Unkulunkulu had told this second messenger to tell the people, "Man shall die!" Well, because the lizard traveled much faster than the chameleon, he reached the people first. When the chameleon finally arrived and told them "Man shall not die," they didn't believe him. They said, "We've already been given Unkulunkulu's message by the lizard, and we believe his message, which arrived first, to be true." Thus the people believed death was inevitable.

As this story conveys, chameleons should be known for their "distractibility" as well as for their changeability.

Possums

The word *opossum* comes from the Algonquian word *wapathemwa* meaning "white dog."

Opossums (Didelphimorphia) are part of a family of mammals commonly found in Australia, including kangaroos, koalas, and wombats. Also called possums, they're the largest marsupials in the Western hemisphere and the only marsupials in North America.

Marsupials tend to be more primitive in their evolutionary development than other mammals. Unlike other mammals, their young develop in an exterior pouch rather than within a saclike membrane called the placenta inside the mother's uterus.

The Virginia Opossum, which is native to the eastern United States, was intentionally introduced into the West by settlers, probably as a source of food. Its range has expanded steadily northward, gradually extending into Canada. Possums have a simple biology, flexible diet, and unique reproductive strategy (explained in the possum sexuality/reproduction section). These characteristics make them successful colonizers and survivors in both diverse locations and varied conditions.

Possum Physical Characteristics

The Virginia Opossum is approximately the size of a domestic cat, with males being larger than females. Baby-faced possums have a pointed pink nose, pinkish coloring, beady black eyes, and rounded "Mickey Mouse" ears. They're slow-moving creatures compared to other mammals their size. Surprisingly, possums have 50 teeth—more than any other mammal.

Most of a possum's body has fur that's white at the base and black at the tip accompanied by long white guard hairs. Possums have hairless feet with opposable thumbs for grasping and a hairless prehensile tail used to grip objects such as tree branches. When young, they can be seen hanging upside down by their tails from tree branches—a commonly known possum ability.

Possum Habits

Possums are opportunistic omnivores, often scavenging other dead animals. Ironically, many possums are killed on the highway while eating road kill, thus becoming the next meal for other scavengers. They also eat insects, frogs, birds, snakes, earthworms, and small mammals. Possums are known to love eating fruit and can become problems in orchards. However, their broad diet allows them to take advantage of almost any food source, including garbage.

Like onions with several layers to peel before reaching the central core, possums have complex qualities that require close observation to understand. They have a remarkably strong immune system and are partially or totally immune to the venom of poisonous snakes. Even with the benefit of being impervious to many diseases and poison, though, a possum's lifespan is unusually short for a mammal of its size. Due to a process called senescence (rapid aging), possums live only two to four years. Senescence is an increased change in the biology of an organism as it ages, which may be due to internal programming by its own genes. (The word *senescence* comes from the Latin *senex* meaning "old man" or "advanced in age.")

As nocturnal animals, they move mostly at night, favoring dark, secure areas. Quiet by nature, only when frightened or threatened do they growl and hiss. When they feel threatened, they first hiss and then show their impressive 50 teeth to scare off attackers. If this strategy doesn't succeed, they pretend to be dead or "play possum"; they won't move at all or even respond to stimuli. In fact, they go through physiological changes similar to fainting in humans. But their metabolic processes continue as if they were totally alert, so they aren't unconscious. This "playing dead" state can last a few minutes up to six hours. This strategy usually encourages an attacker to move on, especially since most predators eat only fresh kills and aren't scavengers.

When playing dead, a possum's lips are drawn back, its teeth are bared, saliva foams around its mouth, and a foul-smelling fluid releases from its anal gland. A possum can be poked, turned over, and even carried away, but it will continue to appear lifeless. Then, when it believes the danger has passed, it moves its ears to pick up any sounds. After that, it moves its head and looks around. If it's no longer in danger, it gets up and continues on its way.

Possum Reproduction/Sexuality

The female possum has a forked vagina with two separate uteri, while the male possum has a forked penis to fit its female counterpart—a significant difference between possums and other mammals. Possum sperm are stuck together in pairs, which helps mobility because a single sperm will not swim straight by itself while a sperm pair does. These biological measures probably evolved to increase the chance for successful fertilization. Also to increase the number of progeny, females copulate with multiple males.

Once fertilization takes place, possum gestation takes only 11 to 13 days. Possums give birth to undeveloped young. From five to ten bumblebee-sized pups crawl into their mother's pouch. Females have 13 nipples, but not all are functional. Only the strongest newborns that are able to reach their mother's pouch and latch on to a functional nipple will survive. Possums often have two litters each year, averaging eight offspring in each litter.

Possums in Myths and Stories

The few ancient stories about possums that exist occur mostly within the Native American traditions and most address how the possum got its hairless tail.

The Cherokee tell a story about how the possum brought the sun back into this world. In doing so, he got so close to the sun that he had to squint, which explains why the possum's eyes appear so scrunched up. While he was busy carrying the sun back into this world, its heat burned off all the hair on its once-bushy tail.

The popular fairytale *Snow White* represents the archetype of the sleeping princess who is not really asleep. She appears to be asleep as a result of a spell cast on her by a poison apple from the jealous aging wife of the king. Snow White awaits the kiss of her beloved prince to free her from "appearing dead." What better animal than the possum to mirror this feigning of death, awaiting a better moment to reemerge and see what might be possible?

Tigers and Other Big Cats

The word *tiger* comes from the Greek *tigris*, which originally came from a Persian source meaning "arrow," referring to the tiger's speed. Besides speed, tigers are known for their power and strength.

Only five tiger subspecies remain alive today. All of them are in danger of becoming extinct due to trophy hunting, illegal Chinese traditional medicine requiring tiger parts, and global destruction of their forest habitat. At one time, approximately 100,000 tigers roamed this planet; today, it's estimated that fewer than 2,500 wild tigers remain. As of 2011, only 59 captive South China tigers are known to exist. Although the Chinese government passed a law in 1977 banning the killing of wild tigers, it was already too late. In South China today, the wild tiger is believed to be extinct.

Tiger Physical Characteristics

Unlike the full-voiced roar of a lion, the tiger's roar sounds like a long snarl and shout. With dagger-like teeth, strong jaws, agile bodies, and pure raw power, tigers are the supreme hunters of the forest and the largest member of the cat family (Felidae). In fact, tigers are the only cat with striped fur, and their stripes don't stop there; if you shaved a tiger, you'd find stripes on the animal's skin as well.

A large tiger might be 10 feet (3 meters) long including its tail, but usually tigers grow to a length of 6 to 9 feet and weigh 350 to 550 pounds (160 to 250 kilograms).

Tiger Habits

Tigers live alone and aggressively mark large territories with their scent to warn their rivals and keep them away. Tigers hunt alone, mostly between dusk and dawn, and often travel up to 20 miles in a night searching for food.

What do they do? First, they silently stalk their prey until they're approximately 35 feet away. Then, with a sudden burst of energy and lightning-fast speed, they rush in to attack. They make the final kill with a powerful bite to the neck or throat of their prey. Finally, they drag their kill to a secluded spot where they can eat in peace.

A tiger eats 30 to 40 pounds of meat in an average night and must make a fresh kill every week to survive. Catching prey is not easy, even for tigers, who are known to be supreme hunters. A tiger might be successful only one tenth of the time. Sometimes they kill domestic animals such as cows and goats; occasionally they kill people. Thankfully, they rarely acquire a taste for humans.

Most cats avoid water whenever they can. However, tigers are great swimmers and love to swim to cool off.

People who live in areas where tigers roam have learned to avoid tiger attacks by wearing a face-like mask on the back of their heads. This works because tigers prefer to approach their prey from behind. They're likely to think twice about pouncing if they believe someone is looking at them face to face.

Tigers and Mankind

In traditional Chinese Medicine, various tiger parts are used as medicine to help manage pain or act as an aphrodisiac. Even though scientific evidence is lacking to support these uses, tigers are still illegally hunted and killed for exorbitant prices to supply this huge market. This, of course, contributes to the danger of the tiger's extermination worldwide. The use of tiger parts in China has been banned; indeed, the government has decreed some offenses in connection with tiger poaching punishable by death.

In addition, all trade in tiger parts is illegal under the Convention on International Trade in Endangered Species of Wild Fauna and Flora. However, a number of tiger farms in China still breed tigers for profit. It's estimated that between 5,000 and 10,000 captive-bred tigers live on these farms today—in contrast to the estimated 2,500 wild tigers left on the entire planet. It's impossible to tell wild tiger parts from farmed tiger parts once a tiger is killed and "processed," thus making enforcement difficult.

Tiger Reproduction/Sexuality

Female tigers or tigresses become sexually mature after two-and-a-half to three years of age and males come of age approximately at five years old. Tiger courtships are minimal, with males and females meeting only briefly to mate. After 100 to 112 days of gestation, normally two or three blind, helpless cubs are born, but female tigers can birth up to six cubs in one litter. The females get no help from the males, which tend to lead solitary lives. Cubs remain dependent on their mothers for 18 months but stay with her for one or two more years before heading out to find their own territory. Adult females generally produce one litter every two years.

Tiger Myths and Stories

In Buddhism, tigers are one of the "Three Senseless Creatures" symbolizing anger. In Hinduism, the goddess Durga is depicted as a 10-armed warrior riding the tigress Damon into battle. In this case, the tiger represents fierceness. Other descriptions? Powerful, fierce, highly intelligent, and solitary.

Lions and other big cats are related but have distinct characteristics.

Lions

The lion (Panthera leo) is one of the four big cats in the genus Panthera, which also includes the tiger, the jaguar, and the leopard.

Lions are the only members of the cat family that display clear sexual dimorphism, which means the males appear far showier than the females. Nature planned well because, being the primary hunter, the female lion or lioness would only be hindered by having such a large showy mane.

With their powerful full-voiced roar, lions are the loudest of any big cat. They usually roar at night and their roars can be heard as far away as five miles or eight kilometers.

Lions are the only cats that live in groups, called prides. The constellation of family members that includes related females, males, and cubs make up a pride. This living arrangement deems the lion as unique as its roar in the Big Cat world, with all others living solitary lives.

Many ancient cultures admired the cooperative hunting strategies of the female lion, as evidenced in many ancient gates that depict lionesses. The lioness rears the young. In fact, when working together, lions learned through evolution to be far more effective in hunting by cooperating with each other. Not only did cooperation lead to more frequently successful hunts but snagging bigger quarry such as elephants became possible.

One of the most well known lion-like creatures, the sphinx, is depicted in both ancient Greek and Egyptian mythology and most famously in the great Sphinx of Cairo, Egypt. With a lion's body and the head of a man, sphinxes have traditionally guarded tombs and treasure, often representing power, riddles, wisdom, and secrets.

In a popular Aesop tale "The Lion and the Mouse," the kind heart of a lion is explored.

Cheetahs

Cheetahs are incredibly beautiful as they run after prey. Remarkably, they can accelerate from 0 to 60 miles an hour (96 kilometers) in three seconds—faster than any other animal on the planet. They're also the fastest mammal alive, actually capable of running 70 miles (113 kilometers) an hour for a short amount of time!

Panthers

Cheetahs are all about speed; panthers are stalkers. In fact, panthers, jaguars, leopards, pumas, cougars, and mountain lions all love to stalk and ambush their prey. Incredibly silent and stealthy, they feel most comfortable alone within their marked territory.

Of all the panther cats, the Black Panther probably has the greatest mysticism associated with it as a symbol of the feminine and the dark of the moon. It represents the power of the night and alludes to death. The Black Panther also symbolizes reclaiming personal power and vanquishing a fear of darkness, death, and fear itself, thus relinquishing the power they embody and hold over humankind.

Porcupines

Porcupine means "quill pig" in Latin. However, porcupines aren't related to pigs; they're actually big rodents!

Porcupines live in most parts of the world and include approximately two dozen porcupine species. All have needle-like quills, which give predators a sharp, painful reminder that porcupines aren't an easy catch.

Not aggressive animals, porcupines don't shoot or project their quills as sometimes believed. In fact, they must have direct contact with another animal to impart their painful quills.

Porcupine Physical Characteristics

A single porcupine could sport as many as 30,000 quills for its defense. Each quill has a sharp tip with microscopic barbs that cause the quills to drive into the muscle of the porcupine's assailant and make them difficult to remove once inserted. Predators and the curious—including dogs and cats—quickly learn that getting too close can result in a nose full of painful quills. Porcupines aren't the worse for wear; they quickly grow new quills to replace the ones they lose in an encounter.

The under-parts of the porcupine have no quills, leaving their soft white underbellies vulnerable. These animals also have the ability to lay their quills flat on their backs so the sharp protrusions won't stick a welcome friend.

Porcupine Habits

Although they live as solitary animals, sometimes they will share a den together, especially during the cold winter months.

Porcupines are herbivores—that is, they eat leaves, twigs, and green plants. They can often be seen chewing on the bark of trees in the winter. To reach new food sources, they often climb trees. Although mostly nocturnal, porcupines sometimes journey out in the daytime in search of food. Attracted to salt, porcupines like the rock salt used to melt ice and snow on roads; they've been known to gnaw on automobile tires coated with rock salt.

Normally "talkative" creatures, porcupines become even more vocal during mating season. Males often fight over females. Female porcupines birth between one and four babies at a time. These babies are born with soft quills that harden within a few days. Most young porcupines are ready to live on their own after only two months.

Porcupines often live up to 15 years.

Porcupine Reproduction/Sexuality

How do porcupines make love? "Very carefully," you may say! The answer is far more bizarre than you might imagine.

First, the male dances for the female, and then he sprays urine all over her head as part of his mating ritual. The final phase of the courtship occurs when the female raises her hindquarters into the air and lowers her chest to the ground. The male porcupine mounts her from behind while holding on loosely but not leaning on her at all. Both porcupines relax their quills, allowing them to lie flat against their bodies. Their intercourse is accompanied by loud squeals, shouts, and whines. Females remain sexually receptive for only a few hours, and then they reject the males.

Porcupines in Myths and Stories

This retold story of how the porcupine got its quills comes from the Chippewa tribe in North America.

Long ago when the world began, porcupines did not have quills, making them highly vulnerable to predators. One day, Bear was walking in the forest and came upon Porcupine. Being hungry, he immediately began to chase Porcupine, who luckily managed to climb a nearby hawthorn tree. Porcupines are excellent tree climbers. *Porcupine* noticed how painful the thorns on the hawthorn tree felt while climbing it, and a wonderful idea came to him. He broke off a branch of the thorny hawthorn tree and tied it to his back.

The next day, Bear again saw *Porcupine* while walking in the woods. This time, rather than run for a tree, *Porcupine* decided to curl up into a ball, exposing the thorny branch on his back toward Bear. When Bear tried to grab Porcupine, he howled in pain and ran away with thorns sticking out of his paws.

Nanabozho (the Creator) saw this and rewarded *Porcupine* for ingeniously creating quills out of the hawthorn branch. To this day, porcupines are covered in quills that protect them from harm. The day after Nanabozho gave *Porcupine* this gift of quills, even Fox got a surprise when he tried to bite into Porcupine.

From this story, you can see that porcupines symbolize having a powerful, prickly defense that protects their sensitive inner beings.

Dolphins

The word *dolphin* originally comes from the Greek δελφίς (delphís; "dolphin," a type of fish) and δελφύς (delphys; "womb") meaning "a fish with a womb."

Marine mammals closely related to whales and porpoises, dolphins live in all the oceans of the world, with 17 different genera including about 40 different species. As carnivores, they eat mostly fish and squid. Among the most intelligent animals on the planet, dolphins have a playful spirit and have always engendered a feeling of friendship among humans.

Dolphin Physical Characteristics

Dolphins range in size from the Maui dolphin—four feet (1.2 meter) and weighing 90 pounds (40 kilograms)—to the Orca, a toothed whale belonging to the oceanic dolphin family—growing up to 30 feet (9.5 meters) and weighing 10 tons.

Dolphins have keen eyesight and can hear extremely high frequencies. They use echolocation (radar) to move through the water and find their prey. It's thought that the dolphin's teeth as well as other facial features work like an antenna to receive incoming sounds. In this way, dolphins can pinpoint the exact location of any object in the water.

Dolphins also have a highly developed sense of touch, with acute sensitivity in their skin, especially surrounding their snouts, pectoral fins, and genital areas. They have no olfactory nerve and hence it's believed they have no sense of smell.

Dolphin Habits

Dolphins spend the majority of their time under water but love to jump into the air. Some species (like the Spinner dolphins) have developed spectacular methods of jumping and spinning at the same time. What a marvel to watch. Playful by nature, they've even been observed surfing in waves for the pure pleasure of it. They freely interact with human swimmers and appear to enjoy playing and communicating.

As social animals, dolphins live in pods usually numbering a dozen. When food is abundant, individual pods can merge, forming mega-pods that include as many as a thousand dolphins. They constantly communicate with each other through clicking sounds, whistles, and other vocalizations. They also emit ultrasonic sounds that help them navigate through the water.

Believed to have kind spirits, dolphins have been observed helping other dolphins that are injured or need to get to the surface and breathe air. They've also been seen protecting human swimmers from sharks by circling around them and even charging sharks head on. Ancient Greek literature includes stories of dolphins helping sailors swim back to shore after capsizing. Some scholars speculate that myths about mermaids began with these stories.

Dolphin Reproduction/Sexuality

Like humans, male dolphins can become aggressive when competing for females or territory. They're known to have sex for the pure joy of it, not only reproduction.

When dolphins exhibit passion, their white underbellies can turn bright pink. They sexually engage belly to belly. Their foreplay can be playful and lengthy, but the actual act is usually brief. They often participate in intercourse several times within a short time and have multiple partners. Approximately a year after conception, a single calf is born.

Dolphins in Myths and Stories

The sense of kinship between humans and dolphins goes back to ancient times. Dolphins have been universally loved and revered in almost all cultures over the centuries. In ancient Crete, for example, dolphins were honored as gods, with a special sanctuary for what they considered to be the dolphin god.

In Greek mythology, Dionysus was said to be captured by pirates who thought he was a wealthy prince they could ransom. When the pirate ship had sailed far out to sea, Dionysus called on his supernatural powers to conjure up vines that covered the ship, mast, and sails. He changed the oars into serpents so terrifying that the sailors jumped overboard. But Dionysus took pity on them and transformed them into dolphins so they'd be able to spend their lives giving help to those in need.

In ancient Greece, Delphin was the dolphin messenger serving the god Poseidon when he was courting Amphitrite. She fled, and Delphin went in search of her, persuading her to agree to marry Poseidon. For Delphin's help, Poseidon placed him among the stars as the constellation Delphinus.

In the Hindu mythology of India, the Ganges River Dolphin is connected to the deity Ganga, the protector of the Ganges.

In South America, the pink Boto dolphins found in the Amazon River are believed to be shape shifters, capable of having children with human women.

The Maoris of New Zealand have a sacred relationship with dolphins and believe that dolphins help them find solutions to difficult problems. They carefully observe dolphins as they swim and can even partially understand their language of clicking sounds.

In modern times, the famous TV series *Flipper* was extremely popular. It continued the ancient belief of how intelligent, kind, and selfless dolphins are in their service to mankind. Today, dolphins are perceived as the epitome of good health, playfulness, and kindness.

Snakes

Snakes can be found on every continent except Antarctica, with more than 456 species being recorded. They range in size from tiny to huge, including pythons that grow as long as 25 feet (7.6 meters).

Many cultures believe that snakes have healing or other powers. The ancient Aztecs worshipped snakes. Quetzalcoatl, the "plumed serpent," was believed to be the Master of Life. In Africa, pythons were worshipped; killing a python was a serious offense. The aborigines in Australia believed that the "rainbow serpent" created all life.

Snake Physical Characteristics

Snakes are long, narrow-bodied, legless reptiles. They're covered in overlapping scales and often have skulls with uniquely hinged jaws, enabling them to swallow animals that are much larger than their heads. As carnivores, they prefer to eat their prey live and whole. Most species are not poisonous.

The scales of a snake—made up of layers of skin cells—provide a protective surface that allows it to move over rough or hot surfaces. The outer cells that are dead protect the living ones underneath. Periodically, snakes shed a layer, leaving behind a snake-like tube of dead skin. During the shedding process, the snake's eyes become cloudy, and for a brief time, it's blind. To shed its skin, the snake finds a sharp edge and rubs against it until the old, dead skin is hooked. Then it easily slides out of this dead shell, revealing its new, shiny skin.

If you've never seen a snake's skeleton, you may wonder if snakes have bones and, if so, how they can be so flexible. Well, they certainly do have bones; the secret to their flexibility is the number and relatively small diameter of them. Snakes have between 100 and 400 vertebrae, with a rib attached to each one of them. This explains why snakes are so flexible and how they can create forward motion. In contrast, humans have approximately 33 vertebrae and 24 ribs.

Snake Habits

When a snake eats, its body stretches to accommodate the size of whatever the snake is consuming. Remember the wonderful children's story *The Little Prince* in which the author draws the picture of a boa constrictor swallowing an entire elephant? Snakes can eat animals many times their size (well, not elephants). The proverbial line, "Don't bite off more than you can chew!" doesn't apply for snakes. They can swallow a huge mouthful, and they don't chew at all. The digestive enzymes break down whatever they've swallowed after it reaches the snake's insides.

Most snakes aren't venomous but enough are to issue caution. Some of the snakes that have venom also have fangs to inject their poison into their prey. Fangs are sharp, long, hollow front teeth connected to small sacs in the back of the snake's head. These sacs produce the venom. When the snake bites, venom gets injected and acts quickly to kill or paralyze the snake's prey.

Venomous snakes are often caught so humans can milk their venom.

Ironically, that venom is used to save the lives of people bitten by the same species of snake. The snake is milked by squeezing its venom sac. This forces the snake to release its poison through its fangs, which have been lodged into a skin covering a glass collection jar. An anti-venom is created from the venom that counteracts the poison.

Snake Reproduction/Sexuality

Snakes employ a wide range of reproductive strategies, although all snakes participate in internal fertilization. The male snake can sense when a female is receptive by the scent of pheromones present. Often the female isn't easily seduced and numerous attempts are required. The male snake has forked hemipenes, which are stored in its tail. The hemipenes are usually hooked or have spines to help hold on to the female's cloaca. Once joined, they are difficult to disengage. Copulation can last from one hour to 24 hours—a whole day—with long periods of stillness.

After the eggs are fertilized internally, most female species of snakes lay their eggs externally, abandoning them to fend for themselves. A few species such as pythons and king cobras stick around and actually protect their clutch of eggs.

Some species of snake retain their eggs internally until they hatch. This happens especially in colder climates to ensure enough heat for incubation. Boa constrictors and green anacondas take this process one step further and nourish their young through a placenta as well as a yolk sac. This is highly unusual for reptiles; it's more frequently associated with mammals.

Snakes in Myths and Stories

In the Judeo-Christian tradition, snakes aren't portrayed favorably. In the Bible story of the Garden of Eden, the serpent's role in "man's fall from grace" has hugely influenced Western culture and thinking.

This foundational myth has also been detrimental to the image of women and to sex itself. In the story of Adam and Eve, Eve listens to the snake and convinces Adam to disobey God and eat from the "Tree of the Knowledge of Good and Evil." The snake initially caused all the trouble between men and women! Because snakes are phallic in appearance, we're led to the notion that sex is evil and will lead to no good. Ultimately, God throws Adam and Eve out of the Garden of Eden and sex becomes the cause of our fall from the grace of God.

In parts of the United States, members of some Christian sects handle vipers with their bare hands as part of a ceremony, testing the depth of their personal faith. In contrast, many other cultures view snakes as powerful, mysterious, and life connecting. The symbol of the AMA (American Medical Association) has two snakes coiled around the staff of life, representing healing, life, and renewal.

Boa and Python Snakes

Boa constrictors give birth to their young live, while pythons lay eggs that hatch. Both pythons and boas kill their prey by constricting them to death and then swallowing their catch whole. Boa constrictors and pythons are known for coiling around their prey and suffocating it. They can weigh up to 60 pounds (27 kilograms).

Rattlesnakes

Rattlesnakes have rattles affixed to the end of their tail that give off a rattling sound when they're agitated. They're vipers, which means they're a species of snake with fangs containing venom that's highly poisonous to humans.

Before they strike with their deadly force, they generally rattle their tails in warning as a first line of defense, so take this warning seriously!

King Snakes

In contrast, the king snake is beautiful and harmless. It protects itself by closely mimicking the looks and markings of its extremely deadly cousin, the coral snake. This strategy of harmless creatures looking like another dangerous species happens commonly in nature. Just remember the old saying that describes the difference in the order of color bands between the two. "If red touches yellow, you're a dead fellow; if red touches black, you're alright, Jack."

Frogs/Toads

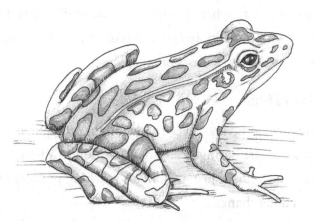

What's the difference between a toad and a frog? Although they're part of the same family, toads are basically frogs that look different because they've adapted to a different environment. But biologically speaking, toads are quite similar to frogs.

Because frogs live in water and are wet most of the time, their skin usually feels slimy. On the other hand, a toad's skin is dry and warty because it spends the majority of its life on land. Thus, toads are identified by their dry, leathery skin, earthy coloration, and the protrusion of wart-like glands as a result of their adaptation to dry habitats.

Another difference is in the formation of the sack in which they lay their eggs: *Frogs* lay their eggs in clumps; toads lay their eggs in lines.

Frog and Toad Physical Characteristics

Toads have short legs, squat bodies, and thick skins with pronounced warts. The warts are actually glands that produce a poisonous milky fluid to protect them from many of their predators. The poison is only harmful if it's ingested or gets in the eyes, but once that happens, it makes any predator quite ill or even causes death. The toxins found in the toad's warty glands have been used for centuries by Native American Indians as well as in Europe for shamanistic purposes.

Contrary to popular belief, toads don't transmit warts to people through contact with the skin. In fact, warts on toads have nothing to do with the virus that produces warts on people.

Frog and Toad Habits

While tadpoles are herbivores because they only eat aquatic vegetation (algae), adult toads are carnivores. This transition in diet parallels the miracle of metamorphosis, just as humans reaching puberty often find their tastes and diets change.

Largely nocturnal, toads and frogs live solitary lives and congregate only at breeding times. In the daytime, toads hide in a variety of cool and moist places such as under rocks and logs or a patch of moist leaves, or they might burrow into the ground.

Toads and frogs love to sing and call out to each other, usually as part of their mating rituals but also as a practical way to find each other in the dark. They give off long trill sounds that can last for up to 20 seconds. As they suck in large amounts of air to sing, they look like puffed-up balloons when they're croaking.

As amphibians, both frogs and toads are capable of living in water as well as on land for periods of time. Frogs have essentially the same traits as toads, but they end up living in the water for their lives rather than on dry land. Grown frogs lose their skins four times a year and their skin peels off in one piece. After it's shed, the frog immediately eats it.

Frog/Toad Reproduction/Sexuality

When frogs sing or croak at night, it's often part of a courtship ritual in mate selection.

Female frogs and toads lay their eggs in fresh water and, for obvious reasons, prefer to find puddles or small ponds that have no fish. Almost all male frogs and male toads fertilize the eggs externally (not inside the female). To ensure fertilization, both males and females participate in a mating posture known as amplexus. The male climbs up onto the female's back and holds on with his forelegs. The pair can remain in this posture for hours or even days as the female lays her eggs. After they're laid and fertilized, the eggs hatch in three to 12 days, depending on the temperature of the water, with warmer temperatures accelerating the hatching time. The tadpoles (babies) that emerge remain as tadpoles for 40 to 70 days. Due to numerous predators, their survival rate is extremely low.

When the tadpoles hatch, they have gills, but as their front legs grow, the tadpoles' gills gradually disappear. They start to develop lungs and soon are able to breathe air. The last two or three days in their development, they complete their metamorphosis and eat insects rather than plants.

The young toads live near their pond of origin for a few more days and then travel in different directions, primarily living on land from that point on. Frogs, however, remain in their birth pond or travel to find a new, larger pool of water to live in.

Frogs and Toads in Myths and Stories

Frogs abound in the mythologies of many civilizations, with myths centering on the frog's metamorphosis from tadpole to adult frog. Universally, cultures see this as a rebirth, thus connecting frogs with creation myths. Frogs can lay up to 3,000 eggs at a time, clearly associating them with fertility deities and creation itself. They also represent the presence of water; many primitive cultures associate them with bringing rain to parched crops.

The Greeks and Romans associated frogs with fertility and the goddess Aphrodite but also with being promiscuous.

In ancient Egypt, the banks of the Nile River would become so overrun with thousands of frogs during mating season that frogs, creation, and birth became linked in the Egyptian mind. Frogs were commonly associated with the goddess Heqet (or Heket), the goddess of fertility and childbirth. Heqet was often portrayed as a frog-woman with a frog's head and a woman's body. Because she was the protector for childbirth, midwives often wore an amulet with Heqet's image on it.

Frogs are frequently found in European myths and fairytales. Two classic lines came into being from the fairytale *The Frog Prince*, representing flip sides of the same ancient archetype: "Kiss me! I'm really a prince (princess)!" and "You have to kiss a lot of frogs before you find your prince (princess)."

In Japan, frogs are often considered symbols of good luck. One myth says that bullfrogs descend from a great ancestor who could suck all the mosquitoes out of a whole room in a single breath. Imagine!

A Curious Mystery Solved

In European as well as early American history, witches were known to have a special affinity for frogs and toads, incorporating them into various brews and spells. Pictures showing witches with large warts on their noses and chins created even more associations to toads. It's a scientific fact that toad warts (as well as some frog skins) contain the chemical bufotenin. This toad venom contains quite possibly the strongest psychoactive substance on the planet—5-MeO- Bufotenin—used by the Apache Indian shamans to create visions and enhance healing. They harvested the milky substance from the Sonoran toad's wart-like glands and then dried it and smoked it. One of the strongest

338

hallucinogens known to humankind, bufotenin can make the participant either extremely high or extremely sick, with death occurring in some cases.

A definite connection exists between how the Apaches and the European witches used toad venom. The witches rubbed the frog/toad skins on their broom handles, then rubbed the bufotenin-treated broom handles between their legs and up into the mucus membrane of their genitalia by hopping onto the broom handles and pretending to fly. Soon they *felt* like they were flying! This practice may have originated the image of witches flying on their brooms, especially on full moon nights. That myth prevails today on Halloween and in popular fantasy stories about witches.

Bufotenin is also found in several species of mushrooms, connecting toads with the name toadstools. Amanitas have wart-like features on their caps that mimic the warts found on toads. Amanita Muscaria, also a hallucinogen, is called the "Divine Mushroom of Immortality." In fact, a book by this title—*Soma: Divine Mushroom of Immortality* by R. Gordon Wasson—is dedicated to the subject.

Odd Frog and Toad Facts

Enjoy these interesting tidbits about toads and frogs:

The main predators of American toads are snakes. No wonder frog and snake archetypes have their share of issues!

The French are closely associated with frogs. A favorite French dish is known as *cuisses de grenouille*, or frog legs, said to taste like chicken. (Doesn't that fit perfectly with genital readings?)

Have you ever heard of the expression "Like frogs falling from the sky"? It's based on actual occurrences in which large groups of frogs (probably during mating season) were picked up by tornado winds in one location and dropped in another.

In ancient Chinese legends, the toad is often a trickster and a magician. Toads are seen as the keepers of the real world and of powerful secrets such as the secret of immortality. This symbolism reflects the miracle of metamorphosis evidenced in the life cycles of frogs and toads. In it, death becomes a metaphor for metamorphosis.

In science, when electricity is turned into photons of light, the change doesn't end there. The energy is transformed into heat and continues to morph into new expressions of energy. Nothing ends; everything is continually transformed into something new. In this vein, life is a "verb" and not a "noun." In fact, nouns don't exist in reality. Frogs teach that there's no such thing as a relationship (noun); there's only relating (verb)—and being present with what truly is.

Turtles/Tortoises

Whats the difference between turtles and tortoises? Turtles spend most of their time in water and have evolved webbed feet for swimming. Tortoises, on the other hand, are land dwellers and have claws rather than webs on their feet. Terrapins, a mix of both, spend time both on land and in water. As true amphibians, turtles, tortoises, and terrapins all have the capacity to dwell on land as well as in the water.

Turtle/Tortoise Physical Characteristics

Turtles come in a huge range of sizes, from the four-inch Bog Turtle to the 1,500-pound Leathery Turtle. They've come to symbolize longevity in many cultures because they can live quite a long time. The oldest tortoise ever documented was Tu'I Malila, a present from the famed British explorer Captain Cook to the Tongan royal family. Tu'I Malila died of natural causes in 1965 at the ripe old age of 188 years.

Turtles have good eyesight and an excellent sense of smell, but neither turtles nor tortoises have teeth. Instead, they have a hard, sharp-edged bone inside their mouths. Their bite echoes that of a bird's beak. Most turtles and tortoises are omnivores, eating both plant and animal foods such as fish, snails, worms, and insects as well as greens, flowers, leafy plants, and even cacti. Some land tortoises, however, are strictly herbivores and eat only plant vegetation.

Turtle shells are uniquely made of 60 different bones joined to make a protective armor that fends off predators. The bones are covered with plates that make the shell even stronger. You might think the turtle's shell has no feeling, but this isn't true. The shell is connected to many nerve endings and turtles can feel your touch through their shells. They can't crawl out of their shells because their shells are permanently attached to their spines and rib cages.

Because the turtle's shell offers such an effective defense against predators, it inspired the creation and use of shields in warfare. Many shields look similar in design and shape to turtle shells, and in some instances, actual turtle shells have been used for shields in battle.

Turtle/Tortoise Habits

When threatened, turtles quickly retract their heads and feet into their shells for protection. This survival strategy works quite well and protects turtles when they're attacked. Having a highly impenetrable shell has helped turtles live as long as they do and thrive as a species.

Turtles/Tortoise Reproduction/Sexuality

Turtle courtship is quite brief and with little drama. It's interesting to note that female turtles store male sperm for a very long time. In fact, they can use one sexual encounter to fertilize sequential clutches of eggs over many months. It's more common, though, for a female turtle to receive sperm from a number of different male donors. When laying their eggs, different males might have fertilized different eggs within the same clutch.

As reptiles, turtles lay eggs and breathe air. All turtles lay their eggs on land. Even sea turtles breathe air and lay their eggs on land in the sand. For some turtle species, temperature determines whether a turtle egg will hatch as a male or a female; low temperatures produce males and high temperatures produce females. Once the turtle eggs are laid, the mother leaves her young to fend for themselves.

Turtles/Tortoises in Myths and Stories

Historically, turtles are symbols of patience and wisdom.

In Hawaiian, the word *honu* means sea turtle and conveys the idea of blessing someone to have a long life.

In North America, Native Americans have a legend about the New Earth being created after a great flood. The legend says the earth we know today was formed on the back of a great turtle, hence the Native Americans named it Turtle Island. The muskrat gathered everything to help create the New Earth and placed it on the great turtle's back.

The Navajo believe turtles symbolize longevity and eternal life. The turtle carries the world upon her back and moves in an unhurried, steady rhythm. She symbolizes the three worlds of water, land, and air.

In Indian Hindu mythology, the world rests on the backs of four elephants and they, in turn, stand on the huge shell of the great turtle Akupara. The giant turtle Kurma is an avatar of the god Vishnu. A temple in Andhra Pradesha is dedicated entirely to Kurmavatara.

In Japan, the great sea turtle Minogame is so old, he's always depicted with a long growth of seaweed trailing behind him as he swims. A favorite motif of wood carvers, he's especially important to the seafaring people of Japan. He also symbolizes longevity and good fortune. Minogame symbols are often seen at weddings to impart blessings to the newlyweds for a long life of good fortune together.

Aesop's famous fable *The Tortoise and the Hare* is perhaps one of the most familiar stories told about tortoises/turtles in Western culture. In this tale, the hare (rabbit) taunts a tortoise about being so slow moving. The tortoise immediately challenges the hare to a race. Of course, the fast rabbit runs far ahead of the tortoise in the beginning, but being overconfident, stops to take a leisurely nap. Meanwhile, the tortoise plods slowly but steadily along, soon passing the sleeping hare, and finishes the race first. The universal teaching in this story exemplifies what turtles/tortoises have come to represent: steadiness, dependability, long life, and good fortune.

Pheasants/Peacocks

The state bird of South Dakota, the ring-necked pheasant, attracts thousands of hunters to the state, providing significant additions to the economy. Ironically, the ring-necked pheasant isn't native to the United States. First brought over from Asia in 1875, it's now well established throughout much of the Midwest.

Peacocks are the most ornate members of the pheasant family, with the male being particularly showy. One might ask, "How can a bird with such conspicuously colored feathers and so burdened down with their weight survive?" Studies on this show that females (peahens) significantly favor males with huge colorful plumage. The brighter the colors and the bigger the array, the better the chance the male peacock will win her attention. Hence, over centuries, peacocks have gone through a natural selection process favoring their attractive qualities. Fortunately, even with their heavy, ornate plumage, male peacocks are still able to fly and can easily reach low-hanging limbs on trees, putting them safely out of reach of the majority of their predators.

Pheasant/Peacock Physical Characteristics

Pheasants are large, colorful, long-tailed birds of the Phasianidae genus. Today, 49 different species of pheasants exist. Native to Asia, these birds have been introduced to many inhabited places all over the world. They tend to have big bodies, long strong legs, four-toed clawed feet, and short stubby beaks. The pheasant's long showy tail, especially evident in the male of the species, is probably the bird's most distinguishing feature.

Pheasant/Peacock Habits

Pheasants are omnivorous, preferring to feed on both plants such as seeds, berries, and acorns and small animals such as insects, earthworms, snails, and occasionally snakes and frogs. They don't migrate; rather, they live their entire lives in one location.

When startled, pheasants as well as peacocks will let loose an ear-splitting shriek. They prefer running when attempting to get away but will take to the air for a short flight into a nearby tree when necessary. Due to their heavy tail feathers and large bodies, pheasants and peacocks can fly for only short distances. However, they're amazingly fast on the ground. They tend to release a loud, bark-like shriek when startled.

Peacocks live for around 15 years in captivity and slightly less time in the wild. Pheasants have similar life spans.

Peacocks

Native to India and Sri Lanka, the peacock is the national bird of India.

Because of their sheer beauty, peacocks have been domesticated for more than 2,000 years and exported all over the world. Best known for their stunning beauty, they're also tasty as game birds for eating. However, in the 16th century when Mexico began exporting turkeys, the peacock fell out of culinary fashion.

Peacocks have a wide range of calls, some bordering on downright eerie.

Peahens nest and feed on the ground but prefer to roost high in the trees, flying up early in the evening before dark, as a defensive strategy against predators.

Pheasants/Peacock Reproduction/Sexuality

Colorful and competitive describes the peacock's courtship ritual. The male peacocks strut around displaying their magnificent plumage, spreading their tail feathers in magical sprays of brilliant colors. They dance about, vibrating their whole bodies in a fast quivering motion, showing off their power and prowess. Female peahens, being quite selective, let only the male they have chosen get close enough to mate.

Pheasant mating rituals are more subdued than that of the peacocks' though male pheasants display their tail feathers in a showy array during courtship rituals as well. Pheasants are polygynous in that the males often mate with three or more females. In fact, they form small harems of female pheasants and remain in the immediate area to protect their young and ward off other males. Once the female pheasant's eggs are fertilized, she visits the nest only once a day to deposit a new egg until the clutch of approximately 11 eggs is full. When the egg-laying process is complete, the female pheasant incubates the eggs by sitting on them. After approximately 23 days of receiving the body heat of the mother hen, the eggs hatch. During this incubation time, the hen rarely leaves her nest. All the eggs hatch within a few hours of each other. Pheasant chicks quickly become self-reliant.

Pheasants/Peacocks in Myths and Stories

A wonderful story comes from Japan about the hero Momotaro who came to this earth inside a giant peach found floating down a river by a kind, childless old woman. During Momotaro's heroic journey, he befriends a pheasant that becomes one of his three helpers. The four of them journey to Megi-jima Island, also known as Onigashima (Ogres Island). With the help of his friends, Momataro overcomes the demon leader Ura and his army of demons. The pheasant in the story embodies the qualities of having goodwill, loyalty, and a strong heart.

The peacock is sometimes known as "the bird of 100 eyes" due to the multitude of eye markings on its tail feathers. The many-eyes motif became a mythic metaphor for the possibility of an all-seeing unfriendly witness. This image found its way into the ancient myths of Egypt, Greece, and Rome, where the peacock feather became a symbol of the "evil eye." Today, a peacock feather is cause for suspicion in some parts of Europe.

By contrast, in an Indian brand of Christianity, the all-seeing eyes of the peacock have come to represent benevolence, resurrection, immortality, and a pure soul. In fact, peacocks are known throughout India to be amazing snake slayers and are thought to be immune to snake bites. In Hinduism, the god Krishna wore peacock feathers in his hair.

In ancient China, the peacock represented beauty, power, and divinity. It was thought that a woman could get pregnant merely with a male peacock's glance because of the bird's incredible attractiveness.

Seahorses

The genus for seahorse is Hippocampus. The word comes from the ancient Greek *hippos* meaning "horse" and *kampos* meaning "sea monster." However, these adorable-looking creatures are actually fish.

Within the genus are approximately 30 species of seahorses. Found predominantly in shallow tropical waters, they prefer to live in protected areas within sea grass and mangroves and around coral reefs. Mythology abounds with them; they're believed to be magical creatures in many cultures around the world.

Seahorse Physical Characteristics

Seahorses are boney, but they don't have scales like most other fish. Rather, they have a thin skin stretched over a series of bony plates arranged in a stacked, ring-like formation. Each species of seahorse has a specific number of rings.

Swimming upright, seahorses spend a lot of time floating and bobbing in and around thick sea grass and mangroves. With their prehensile tails, they can often be found clinging to a blade of grass, resting, and just taking in the view.

As masters of camouflage, seahorses can at times turn totally transparent as well as change colors. They're slow swimmers, so being able to blend in with their environment is paramount to their survival. During mating times, the males sometimes change to bright colors to attract willing mates.

Seahorses have long snouts, which they use to capture food. They eat tiny fish, shrimp, and plankton found abundantly in the ocean. Their eyes can move independently of each other, much like those of a chameleon, which can also change colors.

Seahorse Reproduction

Unique in nature, the males of the species carry their young during gestation in a special pouch on their front. During mating, the female seahorse lays her eggs into the male's pouch that he then fertilizes externally. The male seahorse carries the eggs in his pouch until they're mature, and then he releases the fully developed, independent baby seahorses into the ocean.

In courtship, seahorse pairs move in unison with each other in a kind of courtship dance. It's believed that this courtship dance helps attune the mating pair for the successful transfer of the precious eggs from the female into the male seahorse's pouch. As the ocean is always moving and undulating, this transfer could be disastrous if the male and female don't move in sync with each other.

The male seahorse supplies the eggs with prolactin, the same hormone involved in the production of milk in mammals. At the end of gestation, the male releases an average of 100 to 200 baby seahorses—usually at night to help ensure the survival of the young. By morning, the male seahorse is ready to mate again.

Having the male carry the eggs during gestation allows the female to develop new eggs faster, hence ensuring shorter birthing cycles and better survival for the species. Because seahorses are food for many predators, having a large population helps ensure their survival.

Seahorses and Mankind

In recent times, the greatest threat to the seahorse has been man! Seahorse populations are becoming more endangered in recent years due to over fishing and habitat destruction. Also, the seahorse is a common ingredient in traditional Chinese medicine, with as many as 20 million seahorses killed each year and sold for this purpose. Seahorses are also used for medicine by many other racial and ethnic groups around the world. Specifically, they're used to treat impotence and urinary incontinence as well as enliven the blood, aid in circulation, and alleviate pain from congealed blood and swelling due to sores and boils.

Although seahorses have been used medically for thousands of years, due to modern harvesting technology and increased demand, they're more at risk than ever before.

Seahorse Sexuality

During courtship, the mating pair of seahorses often change to bright colors and swim side by side holding tails. They hold on to the same strand of sea grass with their prehensile tails and spin around in unison in what is known as a pre-dawn dance. They eventually start the final stage of their courtship, which lasts around eight hours. The male seahorse pumps water through his egg pouch, which expands and opens, displaying his readiness. The female seahorse then carefully deposits her eggs into the male seahorse's pouch, where they remain for two to three weeks until maturity.

At one time, it was thought that seahorses were monogamous. Researchers today believe that monogamy does occur, but female seahorses have also been seen mating with different males.

Seahorses in Myths and Stories

In China, seahorses are believed to be a type of sea dragon and, as such, are revered for their power. They're also symbols of good luck.

Ancient Greeks and Romans believed the seahorse symbolized strength and power—qualities attributed to the sea god Neptune/Poseidon.

Ancient Europeans believed the seahorse would carry the souls of dead sailors to the underworld, giving them safe passage and protection.

Seahorses often decorate young people's bodies as preferred tattoos because they conjure up images of magic, beauty, and grace.

Preview: Two Follow-up Books

The Second Book

The second book of this *Signs of Intimacy* series will explore the 48 Love Positions in depth in a card deck and book format. Each of the 48 different Love Positions will have its own card, for which the book provides an in-depth corresponding explanation. The book will not only explore the animal totem behaviors that relate to each Love Position but also provide a detailed description of the energetic and sexual qualities involved.

This deep inquiry will help you expand your skill and understanding so you can enjoy being the incredible lover you truly are. Expect the Love Positions card deck to provide countless hours of fun and exploration. Each day, you'll pick a card and explore a new Love Position with your partner, opening to new possibilities and depths of connection. The 12 different animal totem qualities and the four Love Position variations for each will help you expand your awareness and take your lovemaking to the next level.

The Third Book

Once you've explored the 12 different animal totems and their primary and inner attributes, the obvious next question is, "How do all these different animal archetypes get along with each other?" And along with that, "Is this particular person (totem type) right for me?"

From these 12 totems emerge 72 different possible combinations—e.g., *Rhino* paired with *Rhino*, *Rhino* paired with *Elephant*, *Rhino* paired with *Chameleon*, and so on. In deciphering the age-old question "who gets along with whom?" this third book will be valuable in gaining insight about prospective and existing relationships. It will invite you to participate in a deep inquiry into the different combinations.

As an example of what you can expect, here's one of these 72 combinations: *Chameleons* paired with *Chameleons*.

Chameleons with Chameleons

Imagine two beautiful illuminated beings on a Sunday afternoon, late summer, in a sun-dappled, leafy-green park. Unexpectedly, they catch each other's eye. They can immediately see their own beauty reflected in each other. Their skins, reflecting light and color, begin to blend even before they're totally aware of it themselves. A slow parallel smile emerges. They soon find themselves lost in lively conversation about life's mysteries.

Chameleons love beauty and are naturally attracted to each other initially. Physically, they feel well matched in a narcissistic kind of way. Sexually, they will thoroughly enjoy each other, blissfully playing for hours. For brief encounters, this can be fun, but the difficulty arises when a desire for a long-term relationship unfolds.

Chameleons are too much alike!

After the surface attraction wears off, there's not enough staying power to balance each other. They both long for emotional closeness but lack the ability to find it within themselves. As a result, they constantly seek this reflection in others. Feelings of emptiness can settle in if the depth they seek eludes them.

When they reflect each other's brilliance and beauty, fireworks fly in their lively conversations. But when their natural urge arises to morph into other emotional states, they lose their ability to align with each other—and the energy dissipates.

Chameleons hold the magic of a beautifully polished mirror. They thrive on being in the presence of a powerful, grounded persona. They need constancy for their energy to return to so they can sustain a long-term relationship such as marriage.

When two *Chameleons* meet, it's as if two independently rotating mirrors face each other. An infinite cascading series of beautiful images ricochets off one another. At first, this is exciting and captivating. But when the two mirrors rotate and start to turn away from each other, the two *Chameleons* lose sight of each other. Forgetting the other quickly, they can begin to explore and share their energy with someone new. After all, it's the nature of *Chameleons* to shift into new worlds. They can slip into dream states spontaneously.

Chameleons usually do not become fixated; again, it's not in their nature. So it's safe for them to follow their natural attractions and enjoy what's being offered. There is little danger of one or the other *Chameleon* getting hurt from connecting; they both hold the same power to easily shift into their next loving exchange. In fact, after two *Chameleons* have thoroughly enjoyed each other, one might find two chameleon tails left behind in the park's green grass. It's as if they're leaving an offering so they can both move on to their next adventures. As the saying goes, "If you don't bring a sacrifice, you may become the sacrifice yourself."

Chameleon Men with Chameleon Women

He sees the beauty in her that he knows inside himself. She sees the same reflection in him. In the present moment, they feel extremely happy. Communication comes easily, and they have lively conversations about everything.

Sexually, he's attracted to her; she likes what she sees, too. They both love to experiment. Although they enjoy making love in the bedroom, they frequently get excited about discovering new places. Being outside in nature is always fun, but making love in public places and not being seen tops the list. Like two camouflaged chameleons doing pushups together in the forest, phasing in and out of sight by morphing into the background, the two lovers enjoy being public yet invisible. They both like being wild and naughty—and getting away with it.

Problems arise when they are apart because both can easily get distracted by others in their presence. When one returns to check in, the other is still away so she takes off again. He returns and now she's gone. He gets distracted with someone new. She returns and the cycle continues.

How Can You Raise This Union's Vibration?

Clearly, *Chameleons* being with *Chameleons* raises the issue of being too similar. In many ways, this can and does work to their advantage. As reflective beings, when they actively engage with each other, they generate good times. If for any reason they spend time apart due to business or the natural course of events, they can have difficulty finding each other again. In part, this is due to their airy nature. Just like air, their energies tend to go everywhere.

What happens? They naturally reflect aspects of their respective new environments—including those they're spending time with. This can lead to complex situations and misunderstandings that escalate over time. If the drifting apart becomes sexual, things can get messy.

The first step in changing the possible negative ramifications of this union into a positive vibration requires you to become more aware of the natural tendencies of this totem. When you realize that what's happening isn't personal, an opening gets created. You can always choose how far you wish to travel into this opening. Simply seeing the dynamic for what it is gives you a wonderful start.

Being prepared ahead of time can help immensely, too. The more you can recognize the dynamics and witness them as they happen, the deeper you can heal. Eventually, your awareness will identify your natural urge to act out in these deeply ingrained patterns before you take action on them.

Don't try to fix anything; just allow things to arise in their own way. The more you add your awareness and your ability to witness into the mix, the more everything shifts on its own accord. Soon you'll experience lots of "aha" moments!

Remember, never force your partner to participate in working on your inter-dynamics. It's a personal choice. An invitation can be extended, but each person must participate of his or her own free will. Yet, when both parties participate of their own free will and from their natural desires, the healing process accelerates exponentially.

When peering into the dynamic of how life evolves, it can often be seen as a spiral. At times, the coils of the spiral may appear to be lying flat like a circle. Like the flat coils, you may feel like you're just going around in circles, experiencing the same lessons again and again. By adding awareness and your ability to witness your process, the coils of the spiral will, over time, separate again and expand into a spiral. Your healing will grow through your authenticity.

You may never be entirely complete with this spiral. Qualities that once took over your life might continue to faintly whisper to you. But they'll no longer have a grip, and you'll become increasingly free to expand toward incredible new horizons.

The Indian teacher Osho once said, "The only solution to a problem is to realize that there are no problems. If you believe there is a problem, you are already lost." This emphasizes the importance of bringing awareness to any situation and just witnessing it. Any "problem" will therefore fall away of its own accord. Simply *believing a problem exists* constitutes a big part of the problem.

As humans, we are truly an expression of how we think. And herein lies our salvation!

About the Author

Aiden Talinggers was born in New York City, July 24, 1953. After his first year of life, his family moved to the suburbs of White Plains, New York. Back in those days, White Plains was quite rural. Deer would wander into the family's back yard each evening to nibble on lush vegetation and then fade silently into the twilight.

In his early years, Aiden loved nature and would spend countless hours in the neighboring woods. One of his favorite places was a richly populated pond in the middle of a dense beech and oak forest. As a young boy, he befriended many a wild creature. He especially loved the frogs and how they sang so fully with such total abandonment. Intrigued with the pollywogs and how they could transform themselves into frogs, he loved the whole mystery surrounding metamorphosis.

Aiden became fascinated with the plants in the forest as well. Learning to identify the local flora, he made sassafras tea, ate wild greens, and collected exotic wild mushrooms, feasting on gourmet dinners.

In later years, Aiden traveled to the West Coast, living in San Francisco and Northern California. He became interested in community life and developed skills in the art of listening and communication. Connected to the earth, he also spent many years farming and growing organic foods and herbs such as Echinacea for market.

After successfully dealing with a personal challenge of cancer, Aiden became fascinated with understanding more about human nature and how humans create their own reality. Specifically, he studied dark-field microscopy and became an expert in reading blood. This work deepened his experience of seeing how so much of "who we are" is reflected in our bodies. He worked with more than 4,000 cancer patients, helping them understand their own blood as seen through the microscope. Aiden began to notice a correlation in how his clients' thinking and attitudes about life affected the health of their blood. Wanting to better understand this connection, he traveled to India to study.

What Aiden discovered surprised him. Rather than acquiring new knowledge, he found he needed to *unlearn* what he thought he already knew. By releasing the busy-ness of his mind and dropping into a deeper place of being, everything changed! As a result, Aiden's childhood love for nature and the animal kingdom became rekindled.

Signs of Intimacy arose out of a lifelong exploration of the question "What really makes us tick as people?" Looking to the natural world of animals for answers and parallels, Aiden found an infinite source of inspiration and insight.

The father of two beautiful daughters, Aiden currently lives on the island of Maui in the Hawaiian archipelago. His ground-breaking work on genital readings, has launched a new field of exploration – Genitalogy!

About the Artist

David Jimenez is a true visionary. Living on the Hawaiian Islands, David spends much of his time in nature. He loves the ocean and wild marine life. He has a special affinity with dolphins and is known by locals as "Dolphin Dave".

David's illustrations render clear and concise images, yet simultaneously, capture the underlying living spirit. David's sensitive drawings speak volumes directly to the soul.

David is father to two beautiful daughters.

Contact

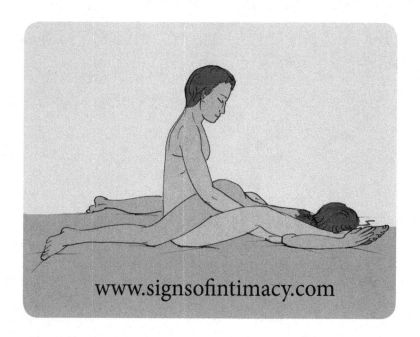

www.signsofintimacy.com

Printed in the United States
By Bookmasters